# POSTCARDS FROM A ROCK & ROLL TOUR

Splendid
BOOKS

Published in 2012 by Splendid Books Limited

Splendid Books Limited
The Old Hambledon Racecourse Centre
Sheardley Lane
Droxford
Hampshire
SO32 3QY
United Kingdom

www.splendidbooks.co.uk
info@splendidbooks.co.uk

British Library Cataloguing in Publication Data is available from
The British Library

978-0-9569505-4-3

Commissioning Editors: Steve Clark and Shoba Vazirani
Coordination: Annabel Silk

Designed by Design Image Ltd. • www.design-image.co.uk

Tour map: Anthony Graham / www.illustrativemaps.co.uk

Photographs: (Pages 20, 40 and 228) Andy Holdsworth
www.andyholdsworthphotography.com

Printed and bound by CPI Group (UK) Ltd, Croydon, CRO 4YY

Gordy's note:
Some of my American readers might think a few of my spellings are incorrect, but as I'm
a Brit I'm using the British way of spelling words like *travelling* and *colour*.

# POSTCARDS FROM A
# ROCK & ROLL TOUR

## GORDY MARSHALL

### FOREWORD BY
### GRAEME EDGE of THE MOODY BLUES

Splendid
BOOKS

*For Susan, Phoebe and Frankie*

# About the author

For the past 20 years Gordy Marshall has toured the world as a musician, playing drums with legendary rock band The Moody Blues. However, it all began at age seven with the start of many years of rigorous classical training on the piano. He started playing drums at the age of 15 and within a short while was playing in local clubs and pubs in his home city of Nottingham. At 22 he moved to London to start a rock band with his friend Peter Howarth. They got a deal and recorded a record but that's as far as it got, so he then put his musical talent to good use and began doing session work.

Since then he's played with a range of artists including Gary Barlow, Lulu, Katie Melua, Sir Cliff Richard and Joss Stone. He also played the arena tours with Justin Hayward, on Jeff Wayne's *The War of the Worlds*. Gordy has performed in many West End musicals including *Fame, Grease, We Will Rock You, Mamma Mia!* and *Thriller Live*.

He has teamed up with hit songwriter Paul Bliss and Peter Howarth of the Hollies to create *Reflections of a Rock & Roll Tour* - a show celebrating the classic hits of the best of British rock and pop. In the past few years Gordy's passion for writing prose has taken hold and he now spends much of his day tapping away at the keyboard, transcribing the many and varied experiences such a life can offer.

He still continues to tour the world with the Moody Blues, and lives in Wimbledon with his wife and two daughters.

# The 2010 Tour

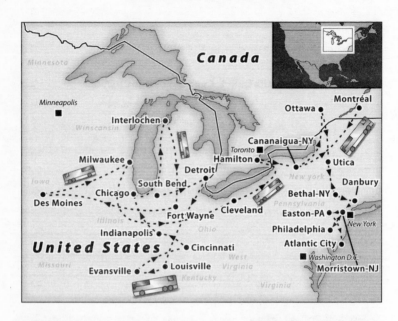

# Contents

# Foreword by Graeme Edge

 Some two decades ago Gordy Marshall appeared in my life. He had stood in for me at a rendering of the British national anthem for an American football game at Wembley Stadium while I was 4,000 nautical miles away on some desperate adventure. Gordy, having stayed sober for the full 12 hours, so impressed Jus and John that they asked him to join me in the engine room of the Moodies for a tour, thus doubling the chances of having a drummer in full charge of his faculties at each gig.

My first public performance with him was in Europe, I can't remember where, but it was not where they eat frogs' legs or sausages. I think they ate herrings, though, so that narrows it down, I hope!

The gig was a great success, and afterwards, backstage, was as people think it is every night. Strange exotic perfumes filled the air and wine flowed freely. I was in my room meditating with a couple of the guys, four girls, a goat, a trombone and several strains of staphylococci, when the door burst open and in ran Gordy. He whispered at about 120 decibels that he could fly, leapt into the air and, for a brief time, he did. However, he then crashed onto the bed,

11

due in part to the fact that the aerodynamic properties of his arms were ruined by the bottles of champagne gripped in each hand, and that the JATO effect he was hoping for was negated by the fact they were both empty. This was a man I could understand.

After performing together for 20 years or more I can say I was right. Playing music together in public will teach you all about the character of your band members, their courage, loyalty and fortitude. All of these characteristics become apparent at times of stress that are due to the little hand grenades life and equipment throw at you.

In this collection of essays that Gordy has written, you too can enjoy his wit, his honesty and his observations of the continuous kaleidoscope that is life on the road. Please read them and enjoy the man as I do.

**Graeme Edge**

# Introduction

In February 1991, when I was still a struggling musician, I had for the longest time held on to the faint hope that one day I would get a phone call that would change my life forever. When the phone rang on this particular day I thought this call might be it.

'Hi Gordon, can you do a gig for me at Wembley Stadium?'

'Wembley Stadium...? er, yes Sarah I certainly can,' I said in a voice that betrayed a rush of adrenalin.

Sarah was the attractive young girl my agent had put me in touch with, and who was now booking me to play at a venue that most musicians only dream of.

'What do you need?' I continued.

'The London Monarchs, London's version of an American football team, are playing a series of games over the coming weeks at the stadium, and I need three drummers to walk around the side of the pitch playing some military drums to get the crowd going,' she said.

My heart sank by the end of her description, so my next words just seemed to slide out effortlessly, 'You mean it's not a gig with the Beatles?' I inquired pathetically, while realising this was not the phone call that would change my life forever.

'What?' she said. 'No, I need you to carry one of those military drums you sling around your neck... oh and do you have a couple of friends, I want one to play the military bass drum and two on the military snares.'

'The ones you sling around your neck?'

'Yes.'

'OK, I can do that,' I said with a marked tone of disappointment.

I then called a fabulous drummer named Ian Thomas, who has since gone on to play with Eric Clapton and Sting and a very good friend of mine, Tony Scantlebury, who played drums for Eddy Grant. I used the same ploy on them.

'Tony, can you play a gig for me at Wembley Stadium?'

The conversation went similarly to the one I had had with Sarah:

'...Yes, one of those drums you sling around your neck.'

The contract was signed and for the coming weeks every Saturday at 2.00pm the three of us walked around the pitch at Wembley Stadium making up funky military grooves, and getting the crowd to clap along in between plays.

At around the same time, this struggling session drummer also received calls to try out for a number of high profile acts. Quite why these should all come up at the same time I don't know, but over the course of a few short weeks I auditioned for Midge Ure, Tears for Fears and even George Michael. I was shortlisted for all of them, but that's as far as I got until one day I was called to do an audition for The Moody Blues.

On a bright and crisp Wednesday morning that same February, I loaded the car with my drums and drove to a recording studio in north London, the name of which unfortunately escapes me.

A man named Mike Keys met me at the door. He was of middling years, dressed in the traditional rock 'n' roll manner of jeans and black T-shirt, with slightly longer hair than mine and a goatee. He helped me in with my drums, and as we set them up he very nicely explained that I was the second of four drummers for that day, and this was day three. The plan was to try out drummers every day of the week and choose the best one. It dawned on me that I was in the middle of what's known as a cattle-call audition. 'Oh well, at least I'll know if I've got this gig by the time I next play Wembley Stadium,' I thought, as I smiled to myself.

Once I was set up Justin Hayward and John Lodge walked in from the back of the studio. The first thing that struck me about the two of them was how tall they both were. Justin had shoulder-length blonde hair – he looked lean and suntanned. John's curly hair was of similar length, and I remember thinking he was dressed in some very expensive looking jeans and had a very firm handshake. The only other person in the room was Bias Boshel, The Moody Blues' keyboard player at the time, who was really smartly dressed in a suit and had more hair than all of us put together. It was a room of musicians for sure.

After running through a number of songs, with each one going really well (I was by now quite used to this audition lark), we eventually moved on to 'Nights in White Satin.' It's quite surreal sitting in a room playing such an iconic song with the people who actually wrote it but with no one else listening. After playing for about an hour, John and Justin thanked me and told me their manager would be in touch. Mike Keys once again helped me to pack my kit up and off I went home.

As I sat on the couch with my wife, Susan, watching television that evening, I wasn't expecting any phone calls. So when Bias phoned I was quite surprised. He said in hushed tones that he wasn't really supposed to tell me just yet, but the rest of the auditions had been cancelled as they had decided to give me the gig. It was to be this phone call that changed my life forever.

There really are no words to describe what a phone call like that actually meant to me. Suffice to say, at age 31 I had been trying to get a gig like this since leaving school. That night we drank champagne.

Cut to the rehearsals. Six weeks of full band rehearsals at the iconic Bray Film Studios. It's where big bands and huge productions take the whole shooting match to rehearse. Huge sound system, full stage monitoring, full crew, catering, offices... the works. In fact as we rehearsed in studio A, Dire Straits were rehearsing in studio B on the same complex. I used to pop my head around the door every time I passed and watch Mark Knopfler and his band play for a few minutes. The following weeks fell into a wonderful routine of Monday to Friday rehearsals with The Moody Blues and then on Saturdays I would quietly take myself on the London Underground up to Wembley to play my American football gig with Ian and Tony without telling anyone.

Then one day it happened.

Halfway through week three of a Moody Blues rehearsal, during a coffee break, John Lodge casually said, 'Gordy, we need you this Saturday at 2.00pm – we have an appearance to make,' with a tone that clearly was expecting a simple 'Yes, OK.'

This, of course, was a problem, especially as I had not told him about my little job on the side, which I was contractually obliged to do.

'Actually I have a... er... Thing on that day.'

'A Thing?' John said

'Yes, a Thing. I don't think I can get out of it,' I offered, hesitatingly.

'What is the Thing? And do you think you could try to get out of your Thing? I'd like you to do a Thing with us,' he said.

'Well, it's just a Thing.'

Realising this tack was not going down well, and of course realising I should make myself available for whatever it was, I followed on quickly, 'I'll call the woman who has booked me for the Thing and get out of it... Incidentally, what's your Thing that you need me for?' 'I don't know what's involved yet, so I'll call my woman now and you call your woman, and let's see if we can sort it out,' he said.

This was in the days before cell phones, so we both walked over to the pay phone hanging on the wall. 'I'll just call first to find out exactly what's involved,' John said.

His phone call ended with something along the lines of, 'Yes... aha... OK. We can do that... Great, see you on Saturday then Sarah.'

Funny that, I thought, my woman is called Sarah too.

John turned to me and said. 'Here's what we need. Can you be at Wembley Stadium on Saturday at 2.00pm? Oh... and you need a snare drum, preferably one of the ones you sling around your neck.' 'If this is a joke, it's really clever,' I thought to myself. 'In fact, that's really bloody clever, how did he just do that?'

Looking like a dog that had just been shown a card trick, it was all I could manage to say, 'Huh? You mean, one of those drums you sling around your neck?'

'Yes, so you can play the drum roll.'

With a look of incredulity and a perplexed tone in my slowly rising voice, I said, 'Would you care to expand on what you're saying?'

'We've been asked to sing the national anthem at Wembley Stadium this Saturday before the London Monarchs game, and I'd like you to stand in the middle of the pitch with us, and play the snare roll – on one of those drums you sling around your neck – and sing it with us,' he said.

For a moment I thought I had been transferred into an episode of the *Twilight Zone*, or maybe I was experiencing some type of parallel universe through an acid flashback? Yes that was it... it must be an acid flashback. There was just one problem with that theory: I'd never taken acid. This had to be the closest thing possible to tripping though, as I just could not get my head around this unquantifiable coincidence.

In this moment I managed one of my more professional outbursts.

'You have to be fucking kidding me,' I said to my new boss.

After I explained the whole thing to him, John didn't seem that surprised. All he said was that when you're on the right track in life, these sorts of things tend to happen. 'You were obviously meant to be here, Gordon,' he said.

It turns out he was correct. After what was originally a nine-week engagement to help Graeme through a difficult patch with his playing following an injury, it turned into a 21-year career (ongoing as I type), that has seen me travel the globe and play on all of the world's most famous stages and TV shows. Graeme and I got on so well and it ended up to be such a blast playing with another drummer, that neither of us wanted it to end. So they just kept booking me for each tour after that.

Quite why I have only just started to write a journal about these most amazing tours, I don't know. It's probably because I've been too busy having the most fun of my life.

So, what you're about to read is a series of personal daily journals. They're more like extended postcards to a friend really, hence the name of the book. I hope this will show you what it's like on a rock 'n' roll tour in the 22 hours we are not on stage. This book is more a personal observation of my travels than a 'kiss and tell,' although there might be a little kissing. I've also delved into the almost limitless supply of Moody Blues coincidences and anecdotes, shooting back in time and recalling some of the more interesting occurrences that have happened over the years. I hope you enjoy it.

**Gordy Marshall**


Follow Gordy on twitter **@gordymarshall**
Find him on Facebook **facebook.com/gordymarshallrock**


---

**The Moody Blues are:**

Justin Hayward
John Lodge
Graeme Edge

**The backing/side musicians are:**

Alan Hewitt (keys 1/vocals)
Norda Mullen (flute/guitar/harmonica/vocals)
Julie Ragins (vocals/keys 2/guitar)
Gordy Marshall (drums)

---

**Postcard 1**

FOR CORRESPONDENCE

FOR ADDRESS ONLY

*Wednesday*
*June 16th*
*2010*

*London, UK*
*to*
*South Bend,*
*Indiana, USA*

Waking up at home in London at 5.30am, a full hour before the alarm is due to sound, I lay in bed with butterflies in my stomach and a distinct feeling of anticipation – an emotion I thought would have long passed, but no. My eyes were wide open thinking of the coming day's events, still not quite comprehending how the next bed I'd sleep in would be in South Bend, Indiana, in the USA.

A while ago, a TV programme about Formula One racing drivers travelling between the US and the UK showed them attempting to overcome jetlag by not eating on the day of a journey. I decided this would be an excellent day to try that idea... but beginning after breakfast. So when my wife and two daughters awoke I was already downstairs making porridge and placing multiple boxes of cereals around the kitchen.

The family sat at the breakfast bar in a melancholy mood because Daddy was about to leave the house for seven weeks. Although I have been doing this for 20 years, the short period of time leading up to my departure never gets any easier. I jovially tried to use the topic of the Formula One fasting as an excuse not to eat, not really wanting to let on that I had a grapefruit-sized lump in my throat preventing me from swallowing anything.

With a few tears and some brave faces, my daughters left for school. Standing on the pavement in my pyjamas, I watched them walk to the end of the road, and together they disappeared around the corner. My neighbour from a few doors away walked quickly past me in a smart suit and said in a jesting tone, 'It's all right for some, lounging around in pyjamas all day.' I smiled at him with my mouth, while my eyes suggested something completely different.

Saying goodbye to my wife was equally difficult, and an 'idiot check' of passport - wallet - phone etc. filled up the minutes to the arrival of the taxi, and the final embrace. This is the hug neither of us wants to end, and there is a type of competition to be the last to let go; however, my mind was already making the necessary emotional shift to rock 'n' roll drummer on tour. It may seem ruthless, but I have to do this as I walk out of the door otherwise I would never leave.

Once I was in the taxi, it took some long gazes out of the window accompanied by a number of heavy exhalations to clear my head. It's an essential seismic shift of emotions, and I was glad that I'm only going on a rock 'n' roll tour and not off to war. In what appeared to be no time I arrived at Heathrow Terminal 5.

John Lodge and Justin Hayward were somewhere around, having begun their journeys from different European cities but I didn't see either of them at the airport, as Terminal 5 is just so huge. And for some reason known only to BA, my frequent flyer card has been cruelly downgraded from silver to blue, which means not being able to access the BA executive lounge to find them, even though my air miles, if they were US dollars, would be able to comfortably bail out Greece.

All of a sudden my stomach started communicating total horror at the prospect of no food for the day. So having agreed with myself to start the Formula One fasting experiment on the plane, I decided it would be prudent to nip into Prêt a Manger and enjoy a quick sandwich. This turned out to be an excellent idea; however when the item arrived, it was the size of a small baseball bat, which certainly satisfied any culinary desires on the plane.

After an uneventful but lengthy flight, we landed on time at Chicago O'Hare airport. This is the point where the American musicians who play with the band are already on the tour bus and waiting to greet the European arrivals.

First up is Norda Mullen, a beautiful, tall, lean virtuoso flautist – also a fourth degree black-belt at Taekwondo – who throws her arms around each Englishman as he boards the bus. Next up: Julie Ragins, our background singer. Slightly shorter than Norda, athletic and blonde, the sort of girl who turns heads in the street every time she exits the bus, Julie is the next to deliver a truly warm American welcome. Then Alan Hewitt, who although slightly older than me looks impossibly young due to a vegan, alcohol-free lifestyle. His enthusiasm for everything in life is utterly contagious, and I can't help but smile broadly in his company as he grips me like a vice.

Graeme Edge, the inimitable founding member of the band who has flown in from his home in Florida gives me a very European kiss on the cheek and a knowing wink for reasons I know not. And lastly Udo Wolf, lovingly referred to as our Glorious Leader, who is simply unassailable in his role as tour manager. He is big, formidable and German and envelops me in a hug which I'm sure has a technical name in the wrestling ring and which, had he not let me go, would have rendered me unconscious in about 40 seconds. Moreover, as we know from past tours, there will be thrills, spills, laughter and tears, with some extreme emotions thrown in for good measure; there is a palpable feeling of expectation in these greetings. On the bus we all share a living space not much bigger than a modest garden shed, for extended periods of time, but with tolerance and the habitual turning of a blind eye we all get on wonderfully... well, most of the time.

Our tour bus and home for the coming weeks is a Prevost; it's one of those huge US rock 'n' roll tour buses that are simply fabulous, with their multi-screen entertainment systems, a kitchen, bathroom and wireless broadband. On this trip, all screens will, of course, be tuned to the 2010 World Cup. In honour of the seemingly limitless facilities aboard this six wheeled veritable palace, I have decided to name our tour bus 'The Good Ship Everything.'

Having refrained from eating during the eight and a half hour flight, followed by an hour or so through customs, then straight into stationary Chicago rush hour traffic, I began to feel rather hungry. It took another four hours to reach the hotel in South Bend. And after my hotel key allowed me into a room already occupied by a rather surprised but nice chap called Michael, I managed to check in. Alan, Norda, Julie and I met downstairs to search for a local place that would serve us food... quickly.

Directly opposite our hotel was the Notre Dame College Football Hall of Fame, which had a small, but rather fabulous, *AstroTurf* American football pitch. We had to cross the pitch to get to the nearest restaurant, and a couple of families were playing with their kids in the humid evening air. What I thought was hunger turned out to be a touch of early homesickness – the scene momentarily pricked a hole in my hard, rock-drummer exterior. 'Not so hard after all,' I remember thinking to myself.

However, that emotion was quickly subdued as Alan caught a passing ball, and he and I started running around pretending to be teenagers - he threw a perfect overhead pass as I ran down the pitch. The kids (aged about seven) seem delighted at our impromptu exercise and ask us to play, until I, not having played American football ever, attempt a rather pathetic underarm (sort of) rugby pass that travelled about six feet before bouncing inconsistently in every direction.

I think they were pleased that we declined their invitation, after my demonstration, and I would have fainted anyway if I had not had food in the following ten minutes.

We found a delightful little place across the street, and enjoyed a surprisingly nice and inexpensive Asian fusion meal with a couple of glasses of red wine. After not consuming any food for nearly 16 hours, the wine hit me like a flying house brick, and something similar to the 'wall' that I imagine marathon runners experience overwhelmed me. My legs felt like lead, my head similar to how I imagine the football felt when I tried to throw it, and my attention span was reduced to less than one sentence at a time.

I returned to my room around 10.30pm. It took less than 45 seconds to undress, take a sleeping tablet and pull the eye-mask (taken from the plane) over my eyes. The sleeping tablet was taken to help guide me through the jetlag-induced, bolt-upright awakening I would normally experience in the middle of the night.

At five o'clock in the morning during my restless, jetlagged slumber, I heard the voices of two men in my room. I cannot begin to describe the feeling of sensing someone breaking into your hotel room. It is a horror beyond horrors, and my instinctive fight-

or-flight reaction kicked in. In an instant I went from a horizontal semi-intoxicated and medicated state to a vertical Kung Fu Panda fighting stance on the mattress of the bed, with adrenaline simply gushing through my veins, while trying to pull the eye-mask off my otherwise naked body.

Simultaneously I heard the loud guffaw of sinister laughter, 'HAHAHAHAAAARGHH!' Not only had these men broken into my room for dastardly reasons that I knew not, but they appeared to find the whole thing deeply amusing. The fear experienced in this moment goes beyond anything I have ever previously encountered. Hyperventilating and panicking, I swung my fists into the blackness of the room, fruitlessly trying to identify the intruders.

Their next utterances however, left me a little confused. 'Welcome to Illinois' premier talk radio station WVPE 88.1FM and a good morning to all you early risers,' came the American-accented radio host's voice.

One of the things I normally always check when going into a new hotel room is that the radio alarm is switched off. The last thing you need when travelling around America on tour is to be woken up at five in the morning by an alarm clock set by the previous occupant of the hotel room. On this occasion I completely forgot to do it, and the previous occupant had left it on full volume.

After having to very quickly visit the bathroom, I am now fully awake and sitting here pleased that my room is indeed secure. Having checked the lock on the door (and the fucking radio alarm clock), I now sit with a green tea in bed writing an account of the last 36 hours.

**Postcard 2**

FOR CORRESPONDENCE    FOR ADDRESS ONLY

*Thursday*
*June 17th*
*2010*

*South Bend,*
*Indiana, USA*

Although I'm writing another postcard today, I doubt it will be a daily occurrence, as I have just got a copy of the itinerary. There are an awful lot of long bus journeys. I can imagine a postcard from the The Good Ship Everything would go something like this: 'Well, I'm sitting on the bus, travelling down the road, and er, well that's it for now, I'll get back to you in six hours!' So I will spare you the minutiae. Yesterday was a little more interesting than that, though...

After finishing the first postcard I made my way down for breakfast, crossing the little football field that was the venue for the previous day's failed sporting attempt, and found a typically welcoming American-style café. I've got to that age where a coffee, everything bagel and a good book will take care of an entire morning.

Sitting in the window of the Chocolate Café, knowing I had four and a half hours before the band was to meet in the lobby for the journey to the venue for rehearsals, I experienced that warm feeling I used to get when sitting down for a good 1950's American movie, normally on Sunday afternoons when I was a child. It's to do with the fact that mostly everyone in America I meet is just so nice... almost annoyingly so. I'm used to the European approach which can often leave the more emotionally delicate customer psychologically scarred for life.

Everyone I've encountered so far since landing in this country has been quite pleasant and helpful, from the rather attractive girl in the military/police uniform at customs, to the receptionist at the hotel, to our bus driver, and then the people serving me in the café. It's that sort of helpful, 'have-a-nice-day' approach, along with a can-do attitude that you encounter over here. I find waiters in Europe can be quite cynical about it. It may be because when asking for a bagel in European cafés, you can on occasions be treated like an armed robber with body odour – or it may just be jealousy. Don't get me wrong: I am not unaware of the darker side of any society, but sitting in this little café in South Bend, everything seemed perfect.

I decided to go for a run along the St Joseph River. The receptionist informed me (very nicely of course) that it was about two miles to the Notre Dame University campus, and it felt like a good idea to make that my destination. Adorned with my running shoes, iPod and rock 'n' roll sunglasses, I embarked on a run for some much-needed exercise. Thus continues the theme of my perfect morning on tour: sunshine, outdoors, and a new place to explore... sublime.

Fifteen minutes into my run along the delightful river, I encountered a series of resplendent properties set back from the riverbank. Each one was statuesque and bespoke in design, set in grounds with grand arches and a perfect view of the river. If only I could cash in my air miles for dollars, I could buy one of these places. As I continued to run, I came across the most beautiful home I think I have ever seen. An exquisite front porch supported handsome, white tree-trunk-sized pillars, which were holding up the front of the imposing building, with a driveway half the size of Texas dividing the sumptuous manicured front garden. Now this is where

I want to live! Forget the air miles – I would sell my grandmother to Aerosmith for this place.

By this point I realised I'd probably been running quite a deal longer than two miles; the river to my left had not been in view for some time and my feet were beginning to hurt. In the euphoria of my post-'everything'-bagel, sunshine morning, happy-with-the-world mood, I had significantly veered off track somewhere and become completely lost. So I turned around to run back.

The return journey proved a little more difficult. I retraced my steps, now not bothering to admire the houses but slightly panicking about the time. No watch... duh! My feet were steaming, and I found myself thinking that everything in America was just too fucking big; why can't everything be closer, like in Europe?

Limping back to the hotel after what felt like half a marathon, but was more likely to be about three miles, I found I had exactly 40 minutes to shower and eat before lobby call. Even though the venue was only 600 yards away, we made the journey on The Good Ship Everything. And before you think this a little excessive, I have to point out we have quite a lot of stuff to transport to the venue. It wouldn't be the coolest thing for a famous rock band to be seen tip-toeing down South Bend High Street carrying a small keyboard, a couple of guitars and a Versace shirt on a borrowed hotel coat hanger, now would it? It might look like we had burgled one of the beautiful houses.

The rehearsal went really well, as it's simply great to sit there and, out of thin air, create something that feels good... although after putting my heart and soul into playing the set through, Justin suggested we do it all again. I nearly fainted at this proposition, but as everyone in the band is meticulous in approach, every song is dissected into its constituent parts, and to this day references are made back to the original recordings to ensure no one has deviated from what they should be playing, we started the set once more from the top.

The whole process was very time consuming, but it is of course, an extremely important part of what we do. Consequently we didn't finish the rehearsal until 9.30pm. Once again I arrived back in my room completely shattered, and was asleep within minutes. This time, however, the alarm clock radio was unplugged from the wall.

**Postcard 3**

FOR CORRESPONDENCE    FOR ADDRESS ONLY

Friday
June 18th
2010

Morris Performing
Arts Theatre,
South Bend,
Indiana, USA

Serie BT 714 v.5

When travelling on tour I simply have to have a good book, whether in hard copy or audio form. This year I have been reading a lot of autobiographies: Richard Branson's *Losing My Virginity*; Peter Ustinov's *Dear Me*; James Caan's *The Real Deal*; and *The Moon's a Balloon*, a lovely book by David Niven — all thoroughly enjoyable reads. However, Rupert Everett's *Red Carpets and Other Banana Skins* is one of the most well written books I have come across in some time.

I was looking for a metaphor to describe performing on stage, as last night at the Morris Performing Arts Theatre here in South Bend was simply awesome. It's a beautiful old theatre that expands out in front of you with open arms as you sit on stage. The whole building has an energy that, together with the audience, is willing you to play your heart out, and is another happy reminder of those 1950's American movies I love so much.

Rupert Everett's depiction of the sensation one gets from performing is expressed in one sentence: 'It's better than drugs, sex or punishment.' It may seem a curious comparison, but really does sum up the experience of performing something that you have worked really hard at mastering, and then having the results judged and commented on by thousands of people sitting in front of you. It's like playing in a winning team every night, which, for this English writer during the World Cup, is quite a novelty.

Speaking of the World Cup, we are driving to Detroit, Michigan today for a concert at the enchanting Fox Theatre (a regular venue for the group), and England are playing Algeria, so all screens on the bus will be tuned to the match. I feel sorry for the three Americans in the band being forced to sit and watch some animated Englishmen shouting utterly fruitless instructions to the players on the TV screen as we trundle along the road towards Lake Erie.

OK, off to the Chocolate Café for an 'everything' bagel, and then back here to pack, which should prove interesting, as my hotel room currently looks like it's been ransacked.

**Postcard 4**

FOR CORRESPONDENCE · FOR ADDRESS ONLY

*Saturday*
*June 19th*
*2010*

*Fox Theatre, Detroit,*
*Michigan*
*to*
*Louisville, Kentucky,*
*USA*

Serie N° 714 C.S

Our venue last night was one of the largest remaining movie palaces from the 1920s: the opulent Fox Theatre in Detroit. It is an utterly breathtaking establishment when viewed from the stage, with a lavish interior featuring a blend of Burmese, Chinese, Indian and Persian motifs. I often think that in order to fully appreciate the wonder of these venues, the audience should be allowed to enter through the stage door to view the auditorium from my vantage point, such is the view.

The Fox Theatre is considered so beautiful that it was designated a national historic landmark in 1989. As if that wasn't enough, the catering backstage was like a five-star restaurant. A local catering company provided lunch and dinner for the crew (ours and local) and band, so after starting with a delicious homemade tomato soup, I helped myself to the whole baked wild salmon (just a portion of course) with a light spinach sauce, green beans, and various salads from the salad bar. I had to leave room for the peach crumble and homemade custard, and then I picked up a small homemade chocolate brownie (OMG, as I believe my children would phrase it) on the way back to the dressing room. I don't think anyone saw me take that, so it didn't count.

Suffering from a 'food coma,' it was all I could do to recline onto a rather plush large red velvet sofa in our dressing room underneath a huge picture of Frank Sinatra, Liza Minnelli and Sammy Davis Junior – a photograph apparently taken in the same dressing room where I lay tranquilised. With a tinge of homesickness, I fell fast asleep. Alan sat quietly meditating and Graeme joined me in a snoring duet (so I am told) from the chair opposite.

While not wanting to create a daily report on how fantastic it is to play the shows on this tour (I am biased, of course, due to the fact that along with Graeme I have the best seat in the house), it's difficult not to enthuse about playing to appreciative audiences. The positive energy we experience on a nightly basis may have something to do with the fact that Graeme, an original member of the band, comes down to the front of the stage during one number, and dances around in white studded jeans to an up-tempo rock song, with an almost adolescent enthusiasm – at age 69. This would have been unthinkable in previous generations.

Of course as a hired musician, it's great pretending to be a rock star for a couple of hours, but I was reacquainted this morning with the inescapable normality of my position, and the fact that I am only a visitor in this land, as I try to order my fourth 'everything' bagel of the tour. We're now in Louisville, and I headed down for breakfast this morning to find an Einstein Bagel Factory. (Before you think I may be in some type of culinary cul-de-sac with my morning food choices, I don't always eat the same breakfast: this is a rare run of bagel consumption. It may be driven by their ubiquitous availability or the fact I don't care about my carbohydrate intake because I burn off all the calories I can take in during the day by playing drums at night.) It took me 20 minutes to order, as the conversation went phonetically something like this:

'Good morning, may I have ay gareen teeee please?' (Spoken with what could only have sounded like the Queen's English.)

'Excuse me?' was the rising retort, with an American accent and look of slight confusion.

'Ay gareen teee with an every... thing bagel and careeem cheese, pleeeease.' (Spoken by me with low-level frustration, but still a smile.)

With a look that suggested she thought I was barking mad, my server said, 'Oh, surrrtainly surr, do you wan' hard warder?'
Now it was my turn to say in a rising tone, 'Excuse me?' as it sounded like an inappropriate proposition.

She now spoke slightly louder and leaned forward with an exaggerated mouthing technique, as if talking to a doddery old man,

'Do you waan haaard waaarder?'

'Oh hot wortter! Yes please.' Phew.

In a tragic attempt at humour I dramatically blurted out a line from Twelfth Night: 'An excellent wench, say I.'

This outburst did not go down at all well.

After wresting the breakfast from my now very pissed-off server, I sat down to eat and contemplated my shocking effort at international relations. I concluded it was much more entertaining to occasionally experience these incidents than not. The bagel was delicious.

**Postcard 5**

FOR CORRESPONDENCE       FOR ADDRESS ONLY

Sunday
June 20th
2010

Horseshoe Casino,
Elizabeth, Southern
Indiana,
USA

Last night's concert took place at the Horseshoe Casino in Elizabeth, which I think is a delightful name for a town. It was outdoors, and genuinely felt more like a summer music festival than a 'casino gig.' Now you may think I am exaggerating the following incident for maximum comic effect, but you would be wrong. It is absolutely true.

After thankfully surviving the frightening experience of my first night here in the US, I inadvertently managed to execute a stroke during the performance last night that I have successfully avoided for 30 years: I hit my face with a drumstick... hard. So hard, in fact, that I saw stars – and they weren't the ones in the sky or on stage. I seriously clouted my right nostril with the acorn (the tip) of the drumstick during the final chord and drum flourish of *I Know You're Out There Somewhere*. After raising my drumstick up from the floor tom-tom (the drum that sits low on my right hand side), in order to hit the snare drum (which sits directly in front of me), my head turned to the right, and I managed to glance my nose with the stick. The strike had the velocity you would normally see in a Bruce Lee movie... but my reaction was more Jackie Chan.

The temperature last night felt positively boiling on stage, I was sweating profusely, and I couldn't work out if the liquid falling from my nose was sweat or blood. There were certainly tears, which would have completed the trio of bodily fluids had a bloody nose been the case (I do apologise for this visual imagery if you are eating). However, it wasn't blood and I managed to compose myself enough to carry on, but it was a little touch and go for a minute.

Sitting here in Louisville on Father's Day, I've just opened the handmade cards placed at the bottom of my case by my children.

They were obviously carefully hidden there when I wasn't looking as I packed back in London, so it was a wonderful surprise to find them this morning. Not because I found them this morning, but because I found them at all. When living out of a suitcase for an extended period, whole selections of clothing are often left in the bottom of the case and never see the light of day. I can endure an entire tour of sartorial choices by going no lower than the first few layers, meaning anything below goes unnoticed. This has, on occasion, resulted in me returning home after the tour and finding unopened birthday cards from weeks before at the bottom of the case.

I am trying to work out the information on today's page in the itinerary, but it's rather confusing. The previous page of the itinerary contains a complicated array of information: address of where we are departing, address of where we are playing and the address of where are sleeping, etc. Not only are they different towns, they are in different states, and all on the same day. I don't know whether it's more confusing to conceptualise a journey incorporating the cities of South Bend, Detroit and Louisville, or the states of Indiana, Michigan and Kentucky. Whichever preferred mental imagery one decides on, it's a daunting prospect, rather like the Three Peaks

Challenge (which involves climbing the highest mountains in Scotland, England and Wales within 24 hours).

If you throw into the mix the different hotel room numbers on a daily basis, or the fact that you might leave your favourite leather jacket hanging in the hotel wardrobe (quite why I brought a leather jacket to this weather I don't know), and the seemingly simple but important fact that the bathroom is on the right in this hotel and not the left, it becomes an unsettling alphabet soup of information.

However, somebody has done a lot of work in organising this well-oiled touring machine, and as long as you hit the main parts of the day, lobby call being the most important, all the rest should follow seamlessly. It's a little like being institutionalised, as we are led by Udo our tour manager and follow only the instructions in the itinerary — which, incidentally, is affectionately referred to as the Book of Lies (BoL), due to its intermittent errors. Occasionally, the BoL will tell us we should be arriving at a Marriott on the outskirts of somewhere named Undergarment, North Dakota, when we're actually pulling up outside the Radio City Music Hall in New York.

In 1994, after arriving at a hotel around 4.00am after an overnight journey in the middle of a very long tour, I walked from the bus to the hotel bed while remaining asleep for the entire manoeuvre. A few hours later, I awoke and after consulting with the BoL, which informed me I was in Des Moines, I obtained a map from the concierge to take a walk. I wandered out into the street to find somewhere to eat. As I ambled along the main street looking at the map while simultaneously allowing my eyes to acclimatise to the blistering summer sun, I noticed the top of the map read Cedar Rapids!

'Stupid bloody concierge has given me a map of the wrong bloody town,' I said out loud on the street, looking around for someone to 'tut' at.

So I strutted back to the hotel and waited impatiently in line to speak to the idiot concierge. When my turn came, I dramatically slammed the map on the desk.

'It might be a help if you gave me a map to the right bloody town mate, this is a map to Cedar Rapids.'

'This is Cedar Rapids,' came the devastating reply.

'What?' said I.

'Where did you think you were, sir?' said the concierge with a sympathetic but ridiculously pleasant tone.

'Er... Des Moines?' I hesitatingly suggested.

'No sir,' he continued, as if talking to a child, 'I can assure you that you, me and everyone else you can see are actually in Cedar Rapids... as stated on the map I gave you earlier.'

'Really?' This response of disbelief must have made me look an even bigger idiot.

With a well-I'm—glad-we-sorted-that-out-then look, I stormed back to my room to confirm what the Book of Lies said. It did indeed say that we were in Des Moines. It turned out that when Jason Raphalian, our then tour manager, had phoned from the bus on the way to the hotel in the middle of the night, there were no rooms at the inn. So he had to divert the bus in the middle of the night to the closest hotel he could find rooms at, which happened to be in Cedar Rapids, 128 miles away. We were all so asleep between bus and bed that no one took the information in, least of all me.

I came back downstairs carrying the Book of Lies, and tried to walk past the concierge desk without being seen, but our eyes met. All I could do was stab my finger at the book as if it was somehow responsible for my behaviour, and 'tut' loudly. I realised later he would have no idea about the BoL, and probably thought I was completely certifiable.

Back to the present day:

I have climbed into bed somewhere in Kentucky (I hope) and will offer another postcard after concluding tomorrow's sojourn encompassing Kentucky, Indiana and Ohio, with a gig somewhere in the middle.

**Postcard 6**

FOR CORRESPONDENCE

FOR ADDRESS ONLY

*The Centre, Evansville,
Indiana USA*

*Sunday
June 20th 2010
(Part 2)*

*to*

*Cincinnati, Ohio.
USA*

The majority of the day has been spent travelling in The Good Ship Everything. Relaxing in my bunk, I watched the movie *Sherlock Holmes*, directed by Guy Ritchie and starring Robert Downey Jr. as Holmes and Jude Law as his stalwart partner Watson. They both engage in a battle of wit and brawn with Rachel McAdams as the love interest. Apart from a hugely enjoyable gig at The Centre in Evansville, along with some extended contemplation of my navel, this has been the sum total of my day.

While lying in my little personal space for this prolonged period, marvelling at how the Japanese have entire hotel rooms in Tokyo no bigger than my bunk, I thought of a little adventure my eldest daughter had about four years ago. She was ten, and on this particular day, along with her little sister (aged eight), she accompanied me into London for a sound check at the Royal Albert Hall. I was playing there that evening with The Moody Blues, and I wanted them both to see the inside of this amazing venue during the day.

The Albert Hall is a notoriously difficult room to amplify properly. I have seen many famous artists play there, and on occasions the sound has been awful. However, Justin knows exactly where the speakers should be and (with the help of Steve, our meticulous front of house sound guy) personally walks around the majestic oval room making sure every seat gets the best mix possible. This process ensures a long day of preparation, with a lot of standing around, strumming guitars, hitting drums and playing grooves.

My daughters' adventure began with a lull in these proceedings. I brought the girls on stage to show them the drum kit, which happened to coincide with Justin checking the sound of one of his acoustic guitars; he was gently strumming a slow rhythm. Quietly I sat my eldest at the drum kit, and as she and her sister have free access to the drums in my studio at the bottom of the garden, they're both adept at playing a basic drumbeat.

Justin wasn't looking behind him as she began to play along. Gently she tapped out a rhythm and after a few bars found her confidence and laid it down. Although her groove was light of touch, it was nice and solid so he assumed it was me and carried on playing. Eventually he glanced around and saw me standing up, then saw Phoebe playing... we all burst out laughing. She had successfully played drums on stage at the Royal Albert Hall, with a bona fide rock star. I don't think she really understood the significance of it at the time, but her adventure – along with a photo of her and her sister Frankie taking a bow to an empty Albert Hall – has subsequently been one of her best show and tell stories at school.

It's been a long day, and at 4.40am on this Monday morning in the second hotel room of the day, I have checked where the bathroom is and unplugged the radio alarm. Along with the help of some remaining jet lag, I think I will be asleep less than 60 seconds after pressing 'save.' Goodnight.

**Postcard 7**

FOR CORRESPONDENCE       FOR ADDRESS ONLY

Monday
June 21st
2010

Cincinnati, Ohio,
USA

On a day off in Cincinnati, I awoke in a hotel room equidistant between the Paul Brown Stadium (home to the Cincinnati Bengals of the National Football League) and the Great American Ball Park (home of the National League's Cincinnati Reds). Only in America could you find two such enormous sporting venues so close together, each one bigger than most European international stadiums.

As the Ohio River runs just south of these colossal constructions, and represents the Ohio – Kentucky border, I wanted to impressively claim that today I jogged all the way from Ohio to Kentucky, and back again. However, I severely underestimated the heat and humidity, so didn't quite manage to reach Kentucky. Instead I jogged down to the Roebling Suspension Bridge, which was built across the Ohio River in the second half of the 19th century.

If you close off any peripheral vision and look only at the bridge, you could almost imagine yourself standing on the banks of the River Thames looking at Tower Bridge, and at first glance you would think the former would be a smaller, quaint copy of the latter.

However, not only is the Roebling Suspension Bridge a lot bigger at 1,057 feet in comparison to Tower Bridge at a mere 800 feet, but it was officially opened on January 1st 1867, a full 27 years before Tower Bridge was opened in June 1894. It's amazing the sort of information you can collect on a Monday afternoon run.

Continuing my exercise east along the north side of the river, I took another opportunity to rest from the heat when I spotted a series of historical markers, which display some quite amazing facts. Did you know, for instance, that the SS Sultana – the boat responsible for the worst maritime disaster in American history – was built in Cincinnati, and most of the estimated 1,800 dead were chiefly from Ohio, just released from Confederate prison camps? That's an awful lot of people...nearly 300 more than died when the Titanic sank.

The day started off in a much less educational but more energetic fashion, however. I woke up at 11.00am, after having agreed the night before to meet John, Julie and Udo in the lobby at 11.15am to share a cab to the local mall. We all wanted to visit the candy store... a.k.a. the Apple store.

After opening my eyes in bed from a prostrate position that, had I been on the floor, would have resembled a dead body, I quickly realised I had only minutes to get from where I was strewn to the lobby. I stopped momentarily in the bathroom to press cold water onto my face in a vain attempt to wake up properly, and throwing on a pair of shorts and a T-shirt – which, once in the elevator, I realised had been extracted from my dirty laundry bag – I found myself standing in the lobby wearing odd socks and jumping into a cab all within seven minutes. My children wear odd socks on purpose, but on me they don't seem quite as hip.

As Bill Bryson pointed out in one of his excellent books, 'We used to build civilisations, now we build shopping malls.' This mall did not disappoint: it was simply huge and had every conceivable shop and service available. Everything really is gigantic in America, and on this day that included our lunch. Udo ordered a dish that would have easily catered for a small Italian village over a holiday weekend, and I'm convinced our waitress got me confused with the football team sitting at the next table.

After attacking my late lunch in a very manly fashion, I am sitting here in the early evening feeling like a beached whale despite a long post-lunch run in the direction of Kentucky. A light supper tonight, methinks!

**Postcard 8**

FOR CORRESPONDENCE      FOR ADDRESS ONLY

*Tuesday*
*June 22nd 2010*

*PNC Pavilion,*
*Riverbend, Cincinnati,*
*Ohio, USA*

I brought with me on this trip a hand blender and a box of protein powder sachets. It saves having to order eggs benedict or yoghurt parfait at 1.00am on room service when I get peckish, and it's a little healthier – with maybe the exception of the yoghurt parfait.

When I opened my case yesterday, I realised the hand blender had been left on the table in the previous hotel. It brought about an expression that requires the shoulders to drop down as far as possible and the head to fall forward with one's mouth slightly open uttering the word 'shit' (or something similar). I didn't do an idiot check before leaving the room; had I done so, I would have realised the idiot had forgotten the hand blender.

So yesterday I called down to the front desk to ask if they could send a blender to my room – an unusual request, I know, but you never know. To my surprise two large men appeared at my door only a few minutes later holding between them what appeared to be one of the machines from the hotel gymnasium. It turned out to be an industrial size blender from the kitchen, which required these two trainee American football players to lift it.

They very kindly placed it on the floor in my room, due to the fact I didn't have a piece of furniture strong enough to hold it. I was rather embarrassed when I knelt down to scoop just a few ounces of protein powder and a cup of milk into the top of it. Thankfully the two young football players had left by this point; presumably they had to go and lie down.

So this morning I went out to buy another hand blender. Our lobby call for tonight's concert was not until later in the afternoon, so there was no rush. While I was meandering around the streets of Cincinnati looking for a shop that sold hand blenders, it dawned on me that crossing the streets in America can be quite dangerous.

You can be standing at a junction with the illuminated palm of a red hand facing you from the opposite side of the street, instructing you not to cross, and not a single car will pass. When you get the signal to walk – an illuminated flashing white stick person – cars which are allowed to turn right on a red light start driving towards you as you're halfway across the road.

I find it puzzling that a country that operates within an infinite array of safety regulations can instruct an unarmed pedestrian to walk into the road, but simultaneously direct a vehicle to drive into the path of said pedestrian. As you approach the far side of the road, invariably something resembling a stylish black tank, but made by Lexus, begins to drive directly at you. You know the vehicle is supposed to stop, but considering the fact that it has blacked-out windows and you can only just make out the silhouette of a driver holding a telephone to their ear, you tend to lose confidence in the principle. There appear to be two types of pedestrians in America: the quick and the dead.

Tonight's concert is at the PNC Pavilion here in Cincinnati, and although I have enjoyed my day off I am now looking forward to getting back doing what we do on tour... playing music.

## Postcard 9

FOR CORRESPONDENCE      FOR ADDRESS ONLY

*Tuesday*
*June 22nd*
*2010*

*PNC Pavilion,*
*Riverbend, Cincinnati,*
*Ohio, USA*

*Serie N° 7/++8*

I've just got in from playing a fabulous concert here in Cincinnati. It was an outdoor gig with high humidity and an audience of similar description. The juxtaposition of the volume and stimulus of the concert, in comparison to the silence and serenity of my hotel room is significant. Sitting here looking at my bed and thinking I should be getting into it reminds me of something...

I'm not sure if the people who run hotels think we're all brainless or if they're just being nice, but they sort of start off the process of getting into bed for you by pulling back the covers and make it look a little like a half-opened envelope, just to make it easier to get in. It puts me in mind of an interesting experience, which occurred after getting into a pre-prepared bed like this after an overnight journey on the bus a few years ago.

We all arrived at a hotel around 5.00am and checked in, still half asleep. Actually our tour manager would have phoned about 30 minutes beforehand, to make sure we were already checked in, and the room keys were ready to hand out. This meant I got off the bus in my pyjamas with a coat over the top, trying to stay asleep. I not only looked like one of the zombies out of the Michael Jackson *Thriller* video, but I was moving like that one on the left.

Lifting open only one eyelid, just enough to identify the room number printed on the envelope containing my room key, I shuffled there like a solo chain gang. Upon getting into the room I purposely did not turn the lights on; I wanted to stay asleep as much as possible. I could see the silhouette of the bed from the digital alarm clock in the corner of the room, but being too tired to unplug it, my shuffling speed increased as I got closer to the bed and, dropping my coat on the floor in my wake, fell onto the corner of the bed that had been pulled back, and returned to my slumber, unconsciously pulling the covers over me.

Several hours later my eyes blinked open; it felt similar to how I would imagine an amnesia patient would awaken. I didn't recognise the room because I hadn't been able to take in any information in the dark at 5.00am. This was not only my third city of the previous day's itinerary, but the third state, and I was slowly going through the common touring thought process of working out where the hell I was.

As I ascended through the various layers of sleep and I became slowly conscious, I also became aware of an uncomfortable viscid feeling on my body. Looking down I could see a sticky substance smeared over my torso and on my hands and arm; it was... well... brown. My initial feeling was one of utter and complete horror, as the worst-case scenario spiralled through my mind. If my worst fears were to be confirmed I would have to swear allegiance to myself never to tell anybody, ever, as long as I lived... never... ever! And I knew I wouldn't be able to even look at myself in the mirror, let alone look at anybody else, if details of this unfortunate incident got out.

I gingerly tested the substance by bringing my hand very slowly closer to my nose, with that same scrunched up facial expression you use when trying to identify whether the 'mud' on the underside of your child's shoe is dog shit or not. It was with complete relief I realised I had fallen asleep on top of that little piece of chocolate left on the bed by the maid, and it had melted during the night.

**Postcard 10**

FOR CORRESPONDENCE

FOR ADDRESS ONLY

*Wednesday
June 23rd
2010*

*The Lawn at
White River State Park,
Indianapolis, Indiana,
USA*

England played Slovenia today at 10.00am in the crucial Group C match in the 2010 World Cup, so I couldn't possibly leave the hotel room to get breakfast. Necessity being the mother of invention, I came up with the perfect middle-aged-rock-drummer-on-tour hotel room breakfast to accompany the match, which required nothing from room service, because I made sure most of the ingredients were included on the rider contract\* from the promoter.

Here's how it's done:

1. *After the gig, collect the berries and fruit from the dressing room and place into one of those ubiquitous large red plastic cups. Incidentally these big plastic cups can also be used to pour your wine into, if you have to leave the venue before you've finished your drink. Then this receptacle is known as a 'traveller.' For this recipe, however, it's known as a fruit and berry carrier.*

---

\* The rider contract on a rock 'n' roll tour refers to the additional requirements of the band other than the fee, to be provided by the promoter. This can mean anything from the amount of bottled water and beers to be in the dressing room, to the type of shampoo and soap in the showers. There are some famously outrageous requests from artists that have become part of modern folklore in the music business, including the dressing room to be freshly painted and a bowl of M&Ms with all the blue ones taken out. It's often just referred to as 'the rider.'

2. Empty one of those small plastic water bottles from the dressing room (preferably Evian), and fill it with skimmed milk. Replace the lid.

3. Put both these items, plus a banana, into your bag before leaving the venue. Try not to look too suspicious.

4. Take one small carton of natural yoghurt from the tour-bus fridge on the way back to the hotel, and place that in your bag before leaving the bus. Now you can't help but look suspicious, but don't worry about it.

5. Once back in your room, place the bottle of milk, the tub of yoghurt, and cup of berries into the ice bucket provided by the hotel.

6. Locate the hotel ice machine (incidentally and quite remarkably there is one of these on every floor, in every hotel in the whole of America), and fill the bucket with ice... around all the ingredients in the bucket, to keep them fresh overnight. Wear shoes when you visit the ice machine, as ice will spill out onto the floor and get your bed socks wet. (Did I just say bed socks? Whoops.)

7. In the morning, ten minutes before the match begins, clean out the ice bucket and put all the cold ingredients – along with half a cup of Scott's porridge oats brought with you from the UK – into it, and, taking a brand-new hand blender purchased the previous day at Macy's, blend together. Then

*pour the contents into the glasses from the bathroom. There will be two of these, and you will undoubtedly spill some of the contents over the sides of the glasses, as they're always too small. Lick side of glass if this happens. Enjoy.*

My World Cup Breakfast Smoothie was consumed while sitting on the bed, watching the match. All I needed was for England to win to complete the morning. In the end the score was 1–0 to England, but I didn't have a good feeling about it. They really didn't look like a championship team to me.

I'm now sitting on the bus as I type this, travelling the 210 miles to Chicago after an amazing show at The Lawn at White River State Park in Indianapolis. John is sitting at the table in the front of the bus reading an historical novel, Justin is sitting right up front next to our driver, David.

For the past three years The Lawn has been named one of the top 100 outdoor concert venues in the world by *Pollstar* magazine, and arriving at this venue, I can understand why. It feels like a proper grown-up gig, the sort of stage you would dream of playing as a budding teenage drummer. If someone had shown me a picture of this place when I was a teenager and told me I would play here one day, I wouldn't have believed them.

The Lawn is situated in the White River State Park, which also houses the Indianapolis Zoo, the Eiteljorg Museum (which presents collections of art, history and the culture of the indigenous Native Americans), the Indiana State Museum, an Imax theatre, and the NCAA Hall of Champions, all set into about 250 acres. This place is breathtakingly vast, and it's so disappointing not having the time to visit all that it has to offer. Mind you, if I had the time to properly visit all the attractions I'm exposed to, I think this little book would be bigger than... well, than it is.

We've only played six concerts, but it feels like we have been on tour an awfully long time. It may have to do with the combination of beds, bunks and sofas I have slept on since arriving, in addition to the number of miles we have already covered. It will be interesting at the end of this leg of the tour to look back and work out how many miles we have travelled, how many states we've visited and how many towns and cities we will have passed through.

**Postcard 11**

FOR CORRESPONDENCE

FOR ADDRESS ONLY

*Thursday
June 24th
2010*

*Chicago, Illinois,
USA*

After travelling yesterday firstly from Cincinnati, then on to Indianapolis for an outdoor concert on one of the sunniest days of the year (lighting by God) with the Ohio River as a backdrop, I am now sitting in a small and rather atmospheric café in Chicago enjoying a late breakfast of a mixed berry parfait, a small panino and a large green tea. I ordered the large tea because this is such a perfect location to write. Yesterday was such a frenetic travel day that I intend to sit here for some time. Incidentally, parfait is French for perfect, which describes my setting.

Parading past the corner window of the café here in Chicago there appears to be an almost continuous stream of beautiful women. Indulge me for a minute and try the following: firstly clench your right fist, and then gently place your teeth around the back knuckle of your first finger. This should give you an idea of the impact of the moving scenery. Opposite is a Bentley garage with a photo shoot of the various sports cars on the street outside with bikini-clad women draped over them. What a pleasant morning!

I've had the pleasure of flying into Chicago numerous times on a private jet in the past, and it has to be one of the most arresting and dramatic nighttime skylines available to anyone travelling on a plane. It's positively Batmanesque in its appearance, and the quite severe banking capabilities of a small jet invites emotions I imagine you would only get while wing-walking. If you happen to be on the 'banking' side looking down at the city, and press your nose against the window, all you can see is a night-lit megalopolis directly below you, with your stomach somewhere above you. It's the ultimate roller coaster feeling.

However, on this occasion we trundled along in The Good Ship Everything (not a poor substitute I have to say), and given the weather, it turned out to be the preferable mode of transport – land turbulence is much preferred to small-jet turbulence to this intrepid but sometimes nervous traveller. I arrived at a newly refurbished and splendiferous hotel in the early hours of the morning, and after a bubble bath of such proportions that it would have fitted perfectly into a Jayne Mansfield movie, I fell asleep into the fifth bed of the tour.

Today is a day off, and as my hands hurt from the force used to hit my drums as hard as possible, it is a much-needed period of rest. I normally only need one day to recover, so the concert at the Ravinia Festival tomorrow should be just as enjoyable as the concert yesterday at the PNC Pavilion.

Before we began the first of our bus journeys yesterday, I once more ran along the Ohio river in Cincinnati, but this time for a particular reason: one of my favourite movies from my youth is George Sidney's 1951 movie *Showboat*, and from the age of eleven I have harboured an almost lifelong dream to be a musician aboard one of these boats.

As there is a paddleboat called Showboat on the river, I wanted to stand close to it for a while, and reflect on my childhood dreams.

Standing there, I experienced a shudder down my spine; although I wasn't exactly working on the boat like my dream, the scene was eerily similar to my youthful imagination.

I once read a book called *Creative Visualization* by Shatki Gawain. The concept of creative visualization is to imagine a situation that you would like to be a reality (in my case it involved a showboat and being a musician), and after descending into a meditative state, you picture the scene in full colour with as much detail as possible, and with all your heart you imagine yourself being there. The idea is that with a bit of metaphysical help (and in my case a lucky break with a famous band), you find yourself in the desired circumstance.

Well blow me over if I'm not standing directly in the middle of my visualization. This is a technique I've used intermittently throughout my life, but in this ebullient moment I am promising myself to revisit the entire concept once more.

We've only been on tour for a week, and we still have more than three weeks to go. I can only imagine what they will bring. It's as though this trip through America is a series of potential film sets, filled with as-yet untold stories.

**Postcard 12**

FOR CORRESPONDENCE

FOR ADDRESS ONLY

*Thursday June 24th*
*2010*
*(Part 2)*

*Still in Chicago,*
*Illinois, USA*

Serie nr 744 6 5

It's amazing what the senses can register in new places. As you travel around your hometown, within a radius of a few miles from where you live, it's easy to become anaesthetised to the sights, sounds and smells which accompany life on a daily basis. This is not the case when venturing out into unfamiliar territory. So, come with me as we take a quick run out of the hotel and down to the waterfront of Lake Michigan.

Exiting the hotel into this urban sprawl that is Chicago, we are first visually hit by an intense cluster of buildings, which appears to have no end, or at least no architectural point upon which the eye can rest. Close to our hotel is the Chicago Water Tower, built in 1869 by the architect William W Boyington, and the John Hancock Centre, one of the most famous buildings of the structural expressionist style. An assembly of further buildings surrounds us with varying shapes and sizes and obscures much of the sky from ground level.

The all-encompassing sound of city traffic takes care of the auditory stimulus, and the olfactory experiences lay just around the corner. We run east along East Delaware Place and turn left onto Michigan Avenue. It's difficult for us to get any running momentum along this road, as there are so many people and of course we have road works that reduce the pedestrian walkway almost to a single file. This is where the first odour hits our nostrils: fresh wet cement. It's not an offensive aroma, but it's equally not something we'd normally expect to find on a main street in Chicago.

We continue to the underpass that takes us to the beach. As we cross the road and descend the steps of the pedestrian underpass of North Lake Shore Drive, the universal and offensive odour of underpasses, stairwells and elevators of old buildings – L'Artisan Coeur de Stagnant Urine – greets us like a very old friend we wish we hadn't bumped into.

As our faces become purple and our cheeks swell, due to us holding our breath for the 60 seconds it takes to sprint through the underpass, we are met with an altogether different experience on the other side – throngs of people scantily dressed in everything from bikinis to sportswear (and these are just the men). With the urban sprawl behind us we now have the full vista of unbroken sky, and the smell of a fresh breeze from Lake Michigan, mixed in with a little burning tarmac – a much more pleasant aroma.

We join a steady stream of athletes cycling, running, skateboarding and walking south along the Lakefront Trail, all travelling faster than us. And as we pass the various restaurants along the promenade, we once again get a varying and fleeting taste of hot dogs, candy floss (called cotton candy in America) and a veritable 'around the world in eighty cuisines' experience on the way south to Navy Pier.

With maybe the exception of Barcelona, I don't know many cities in the world that offer such a cosmopolitan and bustling city life right on the edge of a gorgeous beach. And the similarities with major European cities don't stop here, for as we turn onto Navy Pier we see a giant Ferris wheel which wouldn't look out of place on the River Thames where the London Eye stands, or indeed The Prater, in Vienna, where a giant Ferris wheel built over a hundred years ago dominates the skyline. And all of this within a two-mile radius of my hotel room here in Chicago.

I am finding on many of my jogging sessions that I don't appear to be able to gauge the optimum distance. This makes the return journey much harder than the outward journey. Today is no exception. As a consequence I find myself being overtaken by young and old alike, and now sweating profusely with shirt off I retrace my steps once more along the water, back to the hotel. My focus is now more on my sore feet, rather than the reverse list of edible odours.

I must stop writing now as I am meeting Graeme for dinner in 45 minutes. He's staying in a different hotel, and while making arrangements with him for tonight, he has just informed me on the phone that today he bumped into a fellow musician that he's known for years. They share the same birthday. The musician? Eric Clapton.

**Postcard 13**

FOR CORRESPONDENCE     FOR ADDRESS ONLY

Thursday June 24th
2010
(Part 3)

Chicago,
Illinois, USA

Yesterday ended up becoming more and more interesting and enjoyable as the hours went by. Graeme, Julie and I went to dinner in a local Italian restaurant. We were booked in at 7.15pm, and arriving on time, were shown directly to our table. It's rather early for dinner so there weren't that many people in the restaurant. There was, however, a very long table obviously reserved for a party of about 30 people or more.

After we looked over the wine list and devoured the entire contents of the bread basket, a large party – clearly already underway – entered the restaurant. It was then we realised it was a birthday celebration for the famous guitarist Jeff Beck, and with him were his band. Graeme had already bumped into Eric Clapton earlier in the day, and had seen Sheryl Crow in the elevator. The reason for the gathering of all these stars in Chicago is tomorrow's Crossroads Guitar Festival at Toyota Park. On the bill are Eric Clapton, Stevie Winwood, The Allman Bros. Band, ZZ Top, John Mayer, Sheryl Crow, BB King, Jeff Beck, Jimmy Vaughan, Robert Cray; the list goes on and on. All profits go to the Crossroads Centre in Antigua, a treatment and education facility for drug addicts, founded by Clapton.

As the meal continued I exchanged glances and smiles with a guy at the party who I recognised but couldn't quite place. We had clearly 'clocked' each other as musicians, but as we were at different tables, it didn't feel appropriate to strike up a conversation to find out whom he was. He was middle aged, African American, dressed in very funky attire and was obviously senior in his ranking... you could just tell. Then it came to me – it was one of my favourite drummers of all time, Narada Michael Walden. Not only is he a great drummer, but also a singer, producer and songwriter, and his list of credits include Whitney Houston, Mariah Carey, Aretha Franklin and Diana Ross, amongst others.

As the evening progressed, Narada stood up to toast Jeff Beck, and everybody in the restaurant sang *Happy Birthday*. Following this, five gospel singers came and stood at his table, and, accompanied by a fantastic pianist, sang two songs that were simply breathtaking. It's a tall order to stand there and sing without microphones in front of some of the world's best musicians – I have a feeling these gospel singers may have actually been professional background singers. After this performance, Graeme went over to speak with Jeff Beck, and there were hugs all round. It was then that I got to chat with Narada Michael Walden – it turns out he is playing drums with Jeff Beck. Visits to restaurants like this are rare indeed.

After wiping out a delicious meal and the best part of a bottle of wine, it seemed like a really good idea to me to go and find a jazz club. Of course Chicago is not short of options on this front, but there is a little place I visit whenever we are in town called the Underground Wonder Bar. I went there for the first time nearly 20 years ago, and found myself sitting in with a fantastic funk band back then (the bass player was from the Herbie Hancock band, just to give you an idea of the calibre of musicians who jam there).

As I'm the only real jazz fan in the band, I found myself on my own, and remarkably, as I arrived at the club, the doorman recognised me.

'Hey, Gordy man... great to see you, come on in.'

Is it a good or bad thing to be recognised as a regular in a bar that's not in your hometown? Anyway, last night there was a magnificent, and I mean magnificent, Cuban band playing. My timing was perfect, and as I sat down at the table closest to the stage, they started their first tune.

I don't know what it is about live music, but it really does affect me on some sort of cerebral level. Obviously I play music for a living, but I also listen to it for pleasure; I practice it, I teach it and I will pay good money to go and listen to it live. Sitting in a Chicago jazz club listening to fabulous musicians play music would be the only reason I would go to a bar and drink beer on my own. In my seat right next to the band, becoming ever so slightly intoxicated, I was in my element.

However, there is something about solitary drinking that is different to other forms of social drinking. The waitress seemed to instinctively know when my bottle was empty, and brought me one after another. This continued for about an hour and a half, and it wasn't until I decided to go home that I realised I had drunk more beers than I could count. My head felt perfectly clear, but when I stood up to leave, my body automatically attempted an impromptu impression of Dick Van Dyke in *Chitty*

*Chitty Bang Bang*, when he was pretending to be a life-size string puppet.

I obviously managed to navigate back to the hotel, because I woke up in my bed this morning still holding my toothbrush and wearing only one sock. It was a rather painful awakening, I can tell you, and with my head reminding me that I had maybe drunk a teensy-weensy bit too much. Today has been a slow day, and with lobby call just an hour away, I have to get out of this dressing gown and into the shower.

**Postcard 14**

FOR CORRESPONDENCE          FOR ADDRESS ONLY

*Friday*
*June 25th*
*2010*

*Ravinia Festival,*
*Highland Park,*
*Illinois, USA*

Eighteen thousand people! It's been a while since we had that many at a concert, and it's simply wonderful to play to such a large audience. Tonight's concert at the Ravinia Festival was just awesome. It had quite an intimate feeling to it, as we could see the first 3,000 or so seats really well. The sound onstage was spot on, and the show gained momentum as the evening became darker. It's like a drug with no downside; for two and a half hours all is right with the world.

Thankfully, my hangover from earlier in the day had disappeared before we hit the stage. After the sound check I went to the dressing room, sat down on what looked like a very uncomfortable sofa but was actually quite cozy, and promptly fell fast asleep for an hour.

Alan, Graeme and I shared our dressing room with a Steinway concert grand piano which Alan and I took turns playing. I had quite forgotten how lovely it is to play a Steinway, especially a concert grand. In 2000 I recorded a couple of classical pieces in my studio, one of which was Rachmaninoff's *Prelude in C sharp minor,* and I'm sorry to say that having not played it in a few years, it is now less than note perfect. Anyone passing by outside the dressing room door might have thought there was a dodgy pianist in the band, which, come to think of it, there is: me.

After the show we had some guests backstage, one of whom was radio and TV personality Erich 'Mancow' Muller; he's a huge fan of the band and as well as interviewing the guys on his show from time to time, he always comes to see a concert when we're in town. What's nice about him is that he always comes over to say hello when he sees me. As a backing musician, I like to stay in the background. That means that people often don't know who I am when I'm not on stage, but Mancow always seeks out a handshake and offers compliments. Nice.

John and Justin spent quite a bit of time chatting to him in their dressing room – I could hear extended laughter in the corridor. So, it was some time before we got on The Good Ship Everything.

While waiting I stood at the door leading to the stage to observe the entity known as the crew, who were busy doing what is known in the trade as tearing down. It essentially means getting all the gear from the stage into the correct flight cases, and then onto the two 18 wheel trucks waiting out the back, all done with the efficiency of a pit crew in a Formula One race.

My first contact with an official crew member (or technician as we call them) was when I met Graeme's drum tech, Allan Terry, on the first day of rehearsals in 1991 at Bray Film Studios (the same studios mentioned in the introduction to this book). Prior to the gig with The Moody Blues, the only person to move my drums (or set them up or tear them down) had been me. One sure way to spend time alone is to announce, 'I just need some help getting the drums out to the car,' whereupon everyone from bandmates to spouses runs for the hills.

On the very first day with the Moodies, I pulled up outside the rehearsal studio, which looked to me to be more of an airline hanger. Inside was a venue-sized space with all The Moody Blues gear being set up. The rehearsals began on a Monday and although I wasn't given a specific time, I assumed there would be a 10.00am start. Bray Film Studios are quite a drive from my house, so I began to panic at around 9.45am when I got stuck in traffic, thinking I wouldn't have enough time to get my drums in, set them up and start playing by 10.00am. I needn't have worried.

Flustered, I pushed the door open with my bass drum case, pulling the 'traps case' behind me, walking into a room of silence. John, Justin, Graeme and Ray weren't even there. What I didn't know about this level of gig is that it's not union controlled. You don't clock on at a certain point, and then clock off again at exactly 5.00pm. (This actually happened to me on one memorable occasion, halfway through a piece of music, because the Musician's Union representative insisted on it.) This was a much more laissez-faire approach. Don't get me wrong, everyone was serious about what they did; they just started when they felt it was right. More importantly they did not finish until it was right.

I stood there just inside the door, taking in the sheer hugeness of the room, when a man about five years older than me, in denim shorts and very snazzy trainers, looked me up and down as he drank a cup of tea and said 'Hello?' – it was Allan Terry. I didn't realise it at the time, but Allan's workload had just been doubled with the addition of a second drummer, and he was checking me out. After we both loaded my cases into the jumbo-sized rehearsal room, I pulled out all of my gig-battered drums, which were held together with bits of gaffer tape, and put my equally battered fibre cases to one side. He stood there with his tea and considered the whole sorry collection as one might look at a damaged car. They sounded great (I made sure of that), they just looked like crap. Then he just walked off.

I didn't really know what to make of it all and I began to feel a little intimidated. Then Allan returned with two cups of tea and said, 'Let's have a chat.' I took the tea, and we both stood there staring at my equipment.

Without looking at me and with a smile that tried but failed to reduce the pain of the statement, he said, 'You can't use that pile of shit on this gig.'

'OK?' I said.

'Here's what we're going to do,' he continued. 'This is your drum riser...' he pointed to what looked like a small stage that I'd have all to myself, set into the stage set-up. He took my drum stool and placed it in the middle of my riser and said, 'You sit there.' I did.

He continued more enthusiastically, 'You tell me where you want all the drums to go and I'll build the kit around you.' Then, with his voice a little more animated, 'We'll make a list of all the drums and cymbals you need, all the stands and of course the frame that they all hang off, go and get them, then start building your dream kit.'

'Frame?' I asked. 'Dream kit?'

For the first three days of the first week, and for the first time in my life, I had a bona fide professional drum tech build me a perfect drum kit, with no expense spared. Bit by bit a small urban city of scaffolding and surfaces were erected around me. I don't know who was having more fun, Allan or me. And although I kept on trying to help by moving and lifting things, it always felt like I was getting in the way of his creative process. By day three I had what can only be described as my ultimate Christmas present (but in February), the drum kit of my dreams: two separate snare drums, four tom toms (hanging from the frame), a custom-made 20-inch gong drum hanging up to my right that I would play standing up, four china cymbals in the corners of the 'footprint' of the kit, crash cymbals, bell trees, clamped tambourines, cow bells – in fact, everything that we thought might be used by a percussionist. There was also a drum machine that I didn't know how to work.

At the end of the process, and with various other technicians looking on as they did their things with guitars and keyboards and sound equipment, Allan and I stood back like two bricklayers admiring a wall. Our veritable percussive masterpiece stood there looking like a near full-scale sized version of the Tower of Babel.

Then Allan said, 'Ah fuck.'

'What?' I said. Had we left out some major piece of percussion?

The bass drum maybe? No, that was there. Allan's head fell into his hands. 'What's the matter?' I asked.

'I've got to put this beast up and take it down again every night for the next nine weeks,' he lamented.

'Ooooh,' I said, as my eyes looked away without moving my head. It ended up being a little longer than nine weeks.

I later found out that Allan had previously worked with some pretty big names, including Carl Palmer (of Emerson, Lake and Palmer), Roger Chapman, Peter Gabriel, Robert Plant and Eric Clapton before beginning work with The Moody Blues in 1986, so I was in good hands. He's still mine and Graeme's drum tech to this day.

Back to this day. This group of people work harder than anybody I know, and as well as Allan, there is Mark, our production manager; Jeff, the stage manager; Steve, the front-of-house engineer; Bump on monitors; Neil, our guitar tech; Russ, our keyboard tech; Norman, our audio engineer; Mick, our lighting designer, with his two mates, Jason and Mike; Karen our production coordinator (priceless); as well as David, the driver of The Good Ship Everything. The crew has their own Good Ship driven by Donny, with Russell and Terry driving the trucks. In addition to this there are what appear to be a limitless supply of local crew at each venue to help with the heavy lifting.

Every day these guys (who drive overnight, every night) wake up early in the morning and, straight off the bus, start erecting the stage lights, keyboards, drums, and laying all the cabling, as well as performing a whole plethora of other activities necessary to putting on a show. They are also there for the soundcheck, and obviously all through the show. As soon as the concert has ended, they start to tear everything down, only to do it all once more the following day.

The guitars alone are a full-time job. I have on occasions tried counting them at the side of the stage, but keep losing my place. All the guitars have to be regularly re-strung, tuned and cared for with the greatest attention to detail. When we are playing in the hotter climes tuning can be an issue, so before any guitar is taken to the stage it has to be re-tuned. These men are machines.

**Postcard 15**

FOR CORRESPONDENCE · FOR ADDRESS ONLY

Saturday
June 26th
2010

Chicago, Illinois –
Interlochen, Michigan,
USA to Fort Wayne,
Indiana, USA

Serie Nº 714-C.4

Waking early on the final morning of my short stay in Chicago, I concluded there would be plenty of time for one more run before lobby call at 1.00pm. Setting off again to follow the interesting route of the lakefront trail along the western edge of Lake Michigan, I once more joined the steady stream of athletes perambulating along the water's edge. There was even a group of people cruising along the promenade on those Segway human transporters, those two-wheeled electronic devices you see security guards use in shopping malls. I can just imagine a high-speed chase out of Best Buy on one of those things.

On two separate occasions (once by a Japanese couple, and once by an elderly American couple on vacation), I was asked to take photographs. I concluded two things from these enquiries. First, I must have a 'he-won't-run-off-with-my-camera' sort of face; and second, although I was doing my best Roger Bannister impression, I was clearly travelling at a speed where stationary people could engage me in conversation as I passed by.

As the Ferris wheel once more came very slowly into view, I noticed to the left of Navy Pier an entrance to a park extending out into the water just to the north, and decided to alter my route to take in some different scenery. As I approached the gated entrance, a large sign informed me that the park was dedicated to Milton L Olive III, a US soldier and recipient of the Medal of Honour – the first African American Medal of Honour recipient of the Vietnam war. How very moving, I thought.

I progressed at my normal running speed, reading the sign as I approached, trying to take in the information, and thinking how pleasant this detour looked, when my right foot disappeared into approximately eight inches of mud. 'Shit,' I said, extracting my foot from the swamp masquerading as a footpath. I was now in possession of some rather odd-looking footwear, my left foot sporting a clean white running shoe, my right foot wearing a brown ankle boot. It was going to be interesting trying to pack my trainers into a case later.

Continuing into this serene park on such a pleasant day (foot notwithstanding), I was treated to an amazing view as I looked back from this small peninsula onto the dramatic skyline of Chicago. Dominating the skyline to the right was the John Hancock Centre, and moving my gaze south I could clearly see Water Tower Place, Park Tower, Olympia Centre, and Ontario Centre, continuing along to Sears Tower. This was a most striking and imposing horizon from the Milton L Olive III Park, and in a few short hours I would be treated to a view of the same city from an aeronautical vantage point.

Squelching home turned out to be an uncomfortable business, and after quickly removing my muddy running shoe, I dispatched it inside not one but two plastic laundry bags taken from the hotel wardrobe, before being packed into a case. Then to lobby call where I met The Good Ship Everything, which joined the Chicago traffic for the trip to Midway Airport. I was about to board a brand new eight-seater Citation XLS private jet for two flights, the first being to Interlochen for the next concert.

The 350-mile flight was quick and comfortable, the take-off allowing the aforementioned Chicago skyline experience, but with a landing that made my palms sweat; you really know you are flying in a small aeroplane. Then followed a 30-minute drive to the Centre for the Arts in Interlochen, Michigan.

Interlochen is situated on the northeastern side of Lake Michigan. The Center for the Arts is an all-year-round music college which runs summer camps for aspiring musicians, where they can learn, create and perform with some leading professionals. They also have a fabulous auditorium at the edge of the beautiful, but much smaller, Green Lake. I say small, but Green Lake is about the size of Lake Ullswater, which is the second largest natural lake in England. Green Lake and the similarly sized Duck Lake, just 500 metres to the east, are mere puddles in comparison to the surrounding Great Lakes, of course. The view brought on a momentary feeling of homesickness – or was it travel sickness?

After soundcheck, we were treated to blackened catfish for dinner, which I devoured, perched on a wooden bench in glorious sunshine at the water's edge just 20 feet from the venue. The setting was as near to perfection as possible.

We played to a sellout audience of 4,000, and as most bands find on tour, every show gets better, this one being no exception. Backstage was what can only be described as bohemian, however: no carpets or even dressing rooms to speak of, so although we were comfortable on the sofas provided, the showers were off site in one of the student's cabins – unoccupied by students, I hasten to add.

As soon as the concert finished, one of the runners very kindly offered to drive me to a cabin in a golf cart so I could shower. He enthusiastically travelled through the departing audience at an astounding speed, sending several of them into ditches as we covered the short distance to the cabin. Then he kindly waited for me to finish my ablutions. Thankfully the return journey saw fewer audience injuries, as word had clearly got out that there were a couple of madman running people over in a golf cart.

With a post-shower, fresh-clothes feeling, I ate a rather tasty snack delivered from a local restaurant, and in no time we were all back in the van headed to the airport. There awaited the second golf cart of the day, to take us to the private jet out on the runway. It occurred to me that both of the golf cart chauffeurs I had today must have had the same instructor, as this driver clearly had aspirations of becoming a pilot. He looked rather confused as he took John and I down the runway in the direction of the plane at a speed of somewhere close to 60 miles per hour, and I asked him if he was having difficulty taking off.

Our second flight of the day was 310 miles to Fort Wayne, Indiana. This journey was concluded with less perspiration and a nice glass of chilled white wine, and when we landed at the third airport of the day, our trusty Good Ship Everything was waiting mere feet from the plane, having been driven there while we were busy flying and performing. The day had been extraordinarily well organised, and I entered my hotel room in the early hours of Sunday morning like a kid who had had a very full day at the fair – exhausted but deeply happy. I had survived two daredevil golf cart jaunts, two aeroplane journeys, endured the perils of a shallow mud footbath in Chicago, and arrived in Fort Wayne all in one piece. I will sleep well tonight.

**Postcard 16**

FOR CORRESPONDENCE          FOR ADDRESS ONLY

Sunday
June 27th
2010

The Embassy Theatre,
Fort Wayne, Indiana,
USA

Well, tonight was a rare treat indeed for this musical-theatre-loving rock 'n' roll drummer. We played the Embassy Theatre in Fort Wayne, Indiana. As yesterday was just such a frenetic day of travel and activity, the morning arrived with no audible alarm clock, but rather the more preferable option of waking after just enough sleep – on this occasion, around 11.00am.

I've been to Fort Wayne many times and therefore know something of its history. However, although I'm here for an entire day and night, it comes at a particular point in the tour where the motivation to get out and about is simply not there.

What I can tell you from my memory of previous visits is that it has the nickname Summit City and it's also informally referred to as the City of Churches. This stretches back to the late 1800s when it was the hub of the Catholic, Lutheran, and Episcopal faiths. It has a population of just over 250,000 people, and is the second largest city in Indiana, after Indianapolis.

The historic backdrop notwithstanding, in comparison to previous days, today is a bit of an anticlimax, due to the fact that England lost to Germany in round 16 of the World Cup, and have now been unceremoniously kicked out of the tournament altogether. Considering that we have one German, three Americans and four Englishmen in our little troupe, it makes for very interesting conversation, to say the least. I approached the morning with my customary felicity, but what ended up being the highlight of the day was the homemade granola with blueberries from room service.

Obviously things looked up when I arrived at work, and my eyes fell once more on our historic setting. The Embassy Theatre, where we played, is situated on Jefferson Boulevard and was originally opened in 1928. Our venue this evening offered a capacity audience, which is always a wonderful sight to behold from the stage. It used to be called the Emboyd Theatre and was placed on the National Register of Historic Places in 1975, the same year it reopened as a Performing Arts Centre. It was originally built with an 1100-pipe organ called the Page Theatre Organ, which was fully restored over the 20 years between 1976 and 1996. Remarkably there used to be a seven-storey, 150-room hotel attached, which engulfed the north and west sides of the theatre.

A list of the stars that have appeared at this venue reads like a Who's Who of the American entertainment industry. Louis Armstrong, Tony Bennett, Doris Day, Duke Ellington, Cab Calloway and many, many more internationally known stars have all walked the boards of this historic building.

It blows my mind that tonight I played on the stage where Bob Hope was first employed as an MC. Laurel and Hardy, my all-time favourite entertainers, have also performed here. I find this unbelievable, really. This is the first time I have created a journal listing the venues on a tour of this nature, and researching this information on a daily basis is utterly fascinating to me.

Walking out of the stage door from tonight's concert to hop on the bus back to the hotel, I recognised a couple of the members of the audience standing next to their car, parked next to The Good Ship Everything. They had a red Lamborghini. Being a guy who likes cars but until recently had never owned a decent one, I stood there with my mouth open, slowly drooling, and nonchalantly wandered over to take a look. It was a Diablo, which was the fastest car in production when it was released in 1990. I even managed to have my photograph taken in the driving seat with the doors opened above me, like a huge butterfly stretching its wings.

After we all got back on to the bus, John kicked off a regular humorous theme by saying, 'Does that remind you of your old car, Gordy?' to which everyone burst out laughing.

This rather funny but embarrassing vehicle-ribbing began a long time ago with my really good friend Paul Bliss who played keyboards with the Moodies before Alan Hewitt came aboard. As you would expect, all the guys in the band have really nice cars, Mercedes and the like, and Paul – knowing exactly the unglamorous old car I drove – once asked 'What are you driving these days, Gordy?'

Trying not to laugh and knowing what was coming next, I muttered, 'Oh, you know, just my old Renault 19,' while looking out the bus window, trying to nonchalantly dismiss the question. There were ill-concealed giggles from everyone, as my vehicle inferiority complex was exposed. Then Justin said, 'Gordy, I know how you can double the value of your car,' the answer to which everyone eagerly waited with lips forced together, as he continued, 'Yes... just fill it with petrol.'

These famous musicians found it hilarious.

Then John followed with, 'Hey Gordy, don't leave the windows open – people might think it's a bottle bank.' Cue unconcealed heavy chortling.

The hysterics surrounding my car continued for years... and I mean years. Of course I joined in (you have to). I once announced that I went into a garage and asked for a petrol cap for my Renault 19, and the guy said, 'Sounds like a decent swap.' Paul nearly wet himself.

This recurring theme helped pass the time during countless miles of bus travel. In one tragic attempt at defending my inferior set of wheels, I once offered the simple fact that 'It has a sun roof, you know.' Paul responded without drawing breath, 'Well, don't leave it open – people will think it's a skip.'*

A few years ago on the very first day of a tour, I walked onto the bus and announced, 'I've just bought a BMW so you can all fuck off.' I received cheers and a round of applause from everyone. As the clapping tailed off Graeme murmured, 'That's no good, what are we going to talk about now?'

I am now back in the hotel and sitting here just after 2.00am, thinking about getting into yet another hotel bed. We have a very long journey tomorrow, but more about that another time.

Anyone reading these postcards would not perhaps describe the contents as monotonous, but living this life, it can sometimes feel that way: hotel, tour bus, venue, tour bus, hotel – repeat ad infinitum. It's only when I scratch beneath the surface, and look at these multiple and varied venues of America, in combination with the cities visited and the people I'm travelling with, that I realise what a priceless opportunity I have to explore everything that is offered.

*Although I don't like to explain my jokes, as an American friend of mine didn't know what a skip was, I feel I should explain here that it's a huge open metal container used for builders' waste material.

**Postcard 17**

FOR CORRESPONDENCE

FOR ADDRESS ONLY

*Monday
June 28th
2010*

*Fort Wayne, Indiana,
USA
to
Des Moines, Iowa,
USA*

Today was one of our more glamorous touring days (I'm joking, by the way) – 490 miles non-stop on The Good Ship Everything in pretty much a straight line west, from Fort Wayne, past the southern tip of Lake Michigan to Des Moines, Iowa. The latest city of our rock 'n' roll tour is where one of my favourite authors, Bill Bryson, grew up.

Currently, however, I'm sitting propped up in my bunk on the bus with three pillows, which is rather comfortable. The gentle rumble of the bus is quite soothing, and I have my own little horizontal space with the curtain pulled across. To my right is something that resembles an elephant's hairnet attached to the wall, a sort of giant string-vest pouch, in which you can deposit anything from a bottle of water to a glasses case. In the corner is a circular vent gently letting in air-conditioning, and next to that are two electrical sockets, one of which is powering the computer on which I'm writing.

Directly above my head and behind me is a light that offers just enough illumination by which to read; it has a large plastic on/off knob on the front of it. This makes it easy to find in the pitch black, when you wake up in the middle of the night needing the bathroom.

I have in front of me, attached to the ceiling, a thick but small stylish aluminum device similar in appearance to a dinner tray. Somebody has clearly lain in this position and very cleverly decided that one arm's length is just the right place for such an item. What appears to be a dinner tray is actually a pull-down flat-screen that swivels around at any angle. This is simply fantastic as it means you can lie flat on your back and watch a DVD.

To the left of that, and ever so slightly closer, is a little wooden shelf that looks like it has been pushed through the roof. This is the perfect size for a small tub of dark-chocolate-covered raisins, which coincidentally, is what resides in that space as I write. The only drawback with the shelf on the ceiling is the corners.

On occasions when you wake up in your bunk in the middle of the night, wondering not only where you are, but indeed who you are, and quickly sit bolt upright, with a waking-from-a-nightmare expression - this little shelf comes into its own. The right-hand corner is perfectly positioned to make contact with your forehead. If you happen to inadvertently sit up too quickly in the dark, the impact leaves a small dent in the middle of the forehead, which is soon filled with an amount of fresh blood, rendering the occupant confused and looking rather like a Hindu.

The other potential danger is exiting one of the top bunks. Some people have perfected an almost Olympian-style somersault, landing feet first in the centre of the bus. I don't appear to be that elegant. Apparently, watching me getting out of a bunk in the middle of the night (I have this on good authority by the way) is an event all its own. First, a bare hairy leg appears from beneath the curtain with a scrunched sock on the end, followed by what appears to be a fistfight directly behind the curtain, finishing with an entire body completing a failed swan dive to the floor.

I am slowly coming to the conclusion that being a touring musician is both a merry life and a dangerous one. It may be that as I am a parent, my personal safety gauge has been heightened, with my main concern being keeping my children alive. Or it may be that I become just a little more acquainted with the potential for injury as I get older. I have a distinct memory from not that long ago of considering myself immortal, and would personally and willingly fling myself off the highest diving board, drive the fastest cars and attempt any number of daredevil activities with the presumption of impunity. Now merely alighting from a bunk on the tour bus is fraught with danger. Such is life.

Our destination today is the midwestern city of Des Moines, the capital and the most populous city in Iowa. It's named after the winding Des Moines River, which connects two larger expanses of water to the northwest and southeast of the city, depositing on its route a series of oxbow lakes. While it is one of the major destinations for insurance companies, it also has an impressive list of festivals and events.

We will be playing the Civic Centre in Des Moines on this tour, but in addition to the culture which we are foisting on people, there are many other events including the Des Moines Arts Festival this month, the Iowa State Fair in August, and the World Food Festival in October, as well as The Wild Rose Film Festival, The 80/35 Music Festival, the Celebration Heritage Festival, the Des Moines Renaissance Faire and more. I haven't even touched on the nine museums within the city limits, or the Botanical

Centre, the Blank Park Zoo, the Great Ape Trust with its 230-acre campus, or the Adventureland Park. I wish I were staying longer.

As we approach Des Moines from the east, the 270-foot Iowa State Capitol, with its 23-carat gold leaf dome, is shining like an electric lightbulb in the evening sun, towering above the city. It's the first landmark that indicates we're getting close to our destination.

**Later...**

In order to stretch my legs I walked down Walnut Street and over the bridge in the direction of the State Capitol. As I approached the river I heard a live band playing, and indeed as I looked to my left, on the bridge at East Grand Avenue with the road closed off, there was a live band, smack bang in the middle of the bridge on a mobile stage.

I turned left on to East 1st Street and walked past City Hall on a beautiful balmy evening, and up onto the bridge to watch the band playing. Standing on the opposite pavement (sidewalk, if you prefer), I heard the rhythm and blues waft in every direction, pulling people like magnets to the bridge. There appeared to be some sort of festival going on. What was actually happening was the opening of the brand new Center Street Bridge.

In Newcastle upon Tyne, there is the famous Millennium Bridge, a sort of mini suspension bridge for pedestrians over the River Tyne, linking Gateshead Quay to the quayside on the north bank of Newcastle. The bridge that was being opened this evening in Des Moines looked very similar in design to it. The Des Moines Bridge, although not a suspension bridge, had two curved sections — as the pedestrian approaches the initial crossing he is offered a sort of fork in the road, which joins together at the other end of the link. As the sun went down, the underneath lighting illuminated the swelling water of the river in slowly changing colours. I'm proud to say tonight that I was one of the first people to walk over it, and all while eating a steak and egg burrito from a little food stall I passed on the way.

There were literally thousands of people out in the evening sunshine enjoying the food, music and warm atmosphere of the opening of the bridge and the accompanying Riverwalk. I cannot think of a more congenial and delectable way to end a long day.

However, although I am an experienced 'road warrior,' and used to functioning on my own, I felt (uncharacteristically for me) lonely in this moment. A warm community, celebrating, surrounded me and there was clearly a sense of belonging for everyone. Everyone except, that is, for me. With a shrug, I pulled myself back into the moment. I dawdled pleasantly back to the hotel, managing to enjoy the return journey with improved feelings. All this and I haven't even played a gig here yet.

**Postcard 18**

FOR CORRESPONDENCE     FOR ADDRESS ONLY

*Tuesday*
*June 29th*
*2010*

*Civic Center of Greater*
*Des Moines, Iowa,*
*USA*

Serie B°

I love technology. My oldest friend in the world (and I really mean that) managed to find me via Facebook just before this tour, after us losing contact with each other some 20 years ago. Paul Haines and I were quite literally born together: our mothers were best friends and went through their pregnancies together, and up to 20 years ago our lives were intertwined closely, as we are both musicians.

I chatted with Paul today on Skype from a hotel room in Des Moines, while he was at his home in Wolverhampton in England. Although he now has what we call a 'proper job,' we spent our formative years planning our route to rock stardom. What is it about friends like that? It doesn't matter where you are in the world or how long it's been since last you've spoken; every conversation feels like a continuation from yesterday. When I'm thousands of miles away from family and home, contact like this plays a huge part in keeping me sane.

After writing about the State Capitol here in Des Moines, I decided to use it as a destination for my constitutional run. So donning my current favourite piece of technology – an iPod shuffle – I set off for a run along Walnut Street. Every town in the US appears to have a Walnut Street.

Coincidentally, the book I'm listening to at the moment on my iPod is *Notes from a Small Island* by Bill Bryson, which is about his travels around the UK. As I began to run it struck me as rather ironic that I was listening to Bill Bryson narrate his book as I was running in his home town. Moreover (ironies of ironies), Bill Bryson was talking about being in Blackpool, which is my home town.

Running out of the hotel, ostensibly towards the State Capitol just the other side of the river, I was so taken with this parallelism that I ran 15 blocks in the wrong direction. It wasn't until I was on the outskirts of the city, passing deserted car lots and old warehouses with eroding sidewalks that my error dawned on me.

Castigating myself in the severest terms, I turned on my heel and headed back in the opposite direction. Passing my hotel on the way, I could now clearly see the brilliant golden dome of the State Capitol beaming like a lighthouse in glorious sunshine. This gave me the added momentum I needed to continue. Crossing the river and keeping my destination firmly in my gaze, I began to travel through a more atmospheric part of town.

Noticing a music shop, which was not at all grand from without and looked like it had been plucked directly from 1970, I wandered in to get a break from the stupefying heat. My plan was to pretend to be interested in some second-hand $20 speakers and a second-hand $99 drum kit which was displayed in the window. A music shop with such antiquated equipment could not exist anywhere else in the world, I thought to myself. Moreover, the proprietor was sound asleep, his chin glued firmly to his chest and his long grey hair covering the majority of his middle-aged face. He looked for all intents and purposes as if he had been injected with a general anesthetic. His snoring compared with a lawnmower as he inhaled and a whoopee cushion as he exhaled. He obviously hadn't seen a customer in a while.

I resisted the urge to disturb him, as I really didn't intend to buy anything that day. So I used those few minutes to revisit my youth by looking at all of the old equipment I once could not afford, and then resumed my run, the proprietor never even knowing that I had been in his shop. Perspiring freely, I ran up the regal concrete steps to the entrance of the State Capitol. Now this building is very grand from without and even grander from within. I entered the public entrance on the side, and passed through one of those airport metal detectors, although I don't think it was switched on. Asking if I could look around, a man and woman reclining in comfy chairs and dressed in the traditional security guard's white shirt and black trousers, very pleasantly ushered me through and told me to wander wherever I wished.

My eyes were treated to a magnificent array of decoration, countless works of art and murals as far as the eye could see. I even tagged onto the end of a small guided tour for a while, but as my legs were starting to seize up and I was continuing to sweat profusely, I thought it best to make my way back to the hotel.

Admiring 19th century art in a Midwestern town dressed in a pair of running shorts, a sweaty jogging T-shirt, and sporting one still very dirty Nike running shoe was not the traditional picture of a rock 'n' roll drummer on tour. Surely I was supposed to be drinking tequila and throwing televisions out of hotel windows? The paradoxes made me smile as I ran back out into the brilliant sunshine. On the paved entrance to the building, guys dressed in the traditional roadie uniform of black t-shirts and blue jeans were erecting a huge stage. I briefly stopped on the way back to inquire who was playing. Apparently the Des Moines Symphony Orchestra was giving an outdoor concert here in the next few days. This could have been a scene from any major European capital. Des Moines was really growing on me.

I arrived back at my hotel an hour and 20 minutes after first starting the run, feeling quite exhausted. So I lay on the bed and promptly fell fast asleep, waking up just 30 minutes before lobby call. Why do I always do that? Showering and getting changed far too quickly, I ran to the bus and, with me perspiring heavily once more, we travelled the short distance to the venue.

Tonight's concert at the Civic Centre was a fabulous night. The audience was seated on a steep slope, which meant I could see everybody in front of me. I've been touring with this band for almost 20 years, and the novelty of performing never, ever, ever wears off. The feeling of playing music to enthusiastic audiences is positively exhilarating, and it takes quite some time to 'come down.' After a post-gig shower and donning fresh clothes, sitting with the guys and relaxing with a chilled glass of La Crème is almost mandatory.

The other thing to report in this intriguing and enchanting town is that over the next few days there is the annual Gold Wing Riders meeting of motorcyclists, and they are expecting at least 10,000 attendees – I'll say that again just in case you missed it the first time: that's ten thousand attendees. I've already seen quite a few of these huge contraptions driving around the city, some of them bigger than BMW station wagons. There were even machines with trailers! A motorbike with a trailer – whatever next?

The journey back to the hotel was swift and I now sit in my room feeling pleasantly sleepy, and eyeing the mattress on my bed. I have officially lost count of how many beds I've slept in on this tour.

**Postcard 19**

FOR CORRESPONDENCE      FOR ADDRESS ONLY

*Wednesday*
*June 30th*
*2010*

*Summerfest,*
*Milwaukee, Wisconsin,*
*USA*

According to my father, who is now an American citizen and lives in Maine, the Marshalls descend from a long line of gypsies. Apparently, our family can claim that one of our ancestors holds the most unfortunate of titles as being the last person to be hanged on the Scottish border for horse stealing.

My father (a prosthetist, now retired) has travelled the world extensively over his lifetime, including three years in Vietnam during the war as a volunteer with the Quakers. My brother is a chef and has worked all over the world, and as for me, today I find myself once more visiting three US states in 24 hours. Although I clearly have the easiest job out of the three of us, it appears our family is upholding (at least in principle) its original gypsy lifestyle, but thankfully has ceased the horse stealing and hanging activities. No one can say we don't learn from our mistakes!

On tour in cities like Des Moines, I manage, on occasions, to accomplish up to three exploratory jogging excursions; in others, as in Milwaukee today, the only view to be had was from the inside of a private jet, then a 15-seater van, followed by the inside of a dressing room, ending with a panorama of an audience from a drum kit – then the same again, but in reverse.

This basic description of the day glosses over some rather

interesting facts and figures. For instance, tonight's concert at the Summerfest in Milwaukee is part of the biggest music festival in the world, spread over 11 days, with 11 stages and over 800 bands. On the classic rock stage alone, where The Moody Blues headlined this evening, there were five bands on the bill, with the first beginning at midday. We were the final act on stage at 9.00pm. Usher was playing at the nearby Marcus Amphitheatre (so near, in fact, that we could just about hear him in between songs, and, presumably, vice versa).

The festival, which is also known as The Big Gig, is held at the 75-acre Henry Maier Festival Park on the edge of Lake Michigan. Indeed the back of our stage was quite literally on the waterfront. It normally attracts between 800,000 to 1,000,000 people each year, allowing it to be promoted as the World's Largest Music Festival, a title certified by the Guinness Book of World Records in 1999.

Originally conceived in the 1960s, the Summerfest was inspired by the German Oktoberfest in Munich, and was intended as a similar ethnically themed festival. It continued like that until the Summerfest of 1968, when it began to gain momentum. On this year it was held in multiple locations around the city, and encompassed varied themes including a film festival and even a pageant.

It has continually grown in size over the ensuing years, and in 2008, Harley Davidson teamed up with Summerfest and completely renovated the stage area and increased the footprint of the festival. The opening headliners of some of the years gone by include Bob Hope in 1968, Dolly Parton in 1969, Santana in 1982, Eric Clapton in 1983, Bon Jovi in 1993 and Janet Jackson in 1994. The past few years have included Steely Dan, Stevie Wonder, and Tim McGraw.

My tri-state day began in Des Moines, where the transient

relationship with my latest favourite city was drawing to a close. One last run in the morning, this time in the correct direction, again past the State Capitol, and out to where the houses began to look decidedly less cared for - an area of town for the most part deserted, so I concluded it would be a good place to turn back.

The motorised travel section of the day began with a trip to the airport and aboard the private plane. We were quickly in the air, and before long the gentle hum of our ascension into the clear sky had me feeling rather soporific. Not long after take-off, I was sound asleep with my head leaning to the right, resting with my leather jacket folded on my shoulder, my forehead against the window.

It must have been the optimum power nap, as I slowly emerged from my slumber feeling refreshed. I was gently awakened from my 40 winks with some low-level turbulence; not the type that prompts you to grip the floor with your toes, more a sympathetic nudge letting you know it's time to wake up. I didn't move, I just opened my eyes.

We began a slow and gentle bank to the right, which offered a million details of the painfully bright landscape beneath; I could once again see Lake Michigan. Milwaukee, our destination, is on the west side of Lake Michigan north of Chicago, although on this occasion I wouldn't be seeing much of Milwaukee: we were due to fly out directly after the concert.

The landing was smooth and elegant, and in no time our van was pulling up next to the Classic Rock stage at Summerfest. There was already a band onstage playing at full throttle, and we arrived to a warmed-up audience who were clearly comprehensively refreshed. It was loud and noisy, there were no facilities to speak of – just a trailer with a toilet and sink – and the atmosphere was what could only be described as mildly raucous... I loved it!

We walked on stage at exactly 9.00pm with no soundcheck, having to put our faith completely in the hands of the crew and technicians, who had previously set everything up. After our introduction and the count-in, we started the first song just as the sun was setting. For me, a sense of impending adventure always accompanies these types of concerts, and tonight I was not disappointed.

I don't know how big the crowd was tonight, but from where I was sitting there was a large expanse of audience as far as the eye could see. It's an amazing sight to see a carpet of heads bobbing around in front of you, all in time with your right foot as you hit the bass drum pedal. It's as if the pedal contains a low-voltage electrical charge, and every time you play it, thousands of people in front receive a few milliamps, and they all jump six inches into the air. It's quite surreal.

About 90 minutes later we exited the stage to thunderous applause and walked briskly to the trailer. Changing quickly, we left in the van to try to beat the traffic, and within what seemed like minutes we were climbing into the nighttime sky, en route to the next bed of the tour.

**Postcard 20**

FOR CORRESPONDENCE    FOR ADDRESS ONLY

*Friday*
*July 2nd*
*2010*

*Cleveland, Ohio, USA*
*to*
*Toledo, Ohio, USA*
*(and back again)*

I now find myself in Cleveland, Ohio, home of the Rock 'n' Roll Hall of Fame. Cleveland, as you may know, is considered the home of rock 'n' roll: the phrase was coined by a local DJ called Alan 'Moondog' Freed in the 1950s. Did you know that Moondog, one of the most influential radio personalities of the time, was instrumental in the foundation of Cleveland's early rock 'n' roll heritage through his radio programme, which featured African-American-based rhythm and blues music? He even organised what is considered to be the first rock 'n' roll concert on March 21st 1952, called The Moondog Coronation Ball. The annual concert continues to this day as part of Cleveland's rock 'n' roll historical culture.

Although we are staying in Cleveland, last night's show was in Toledo, Ohio, about 115 miles to the west. The unusual venue of Toledo Zoo is one the band has played on many occasions, and the show is held outdoors in the grounds of the zoo, which accommodates several thousand people. The zoo started out in 1900 as the Toledo Zoological Gardens, and in 1982 ownership was transferred from the city to the Toledo Zoological Society, a private non-profit organisation, which professionalised the zoo's management. Hence the use of the grounds for concerts to help raise money for the zoo. A simply brilliant idea if you ask me.

There is a 200-seat theatre inside the building, and although this venue is too small for The Moody Blues to perform, the stage of this theatre became our ad hoc dressing room for the night. It essentially consists of some hanging curtains and our flight-cased wardrobes with imported furniture. It's the only time I think The Moody Blues have ever disrobed on stage, so to speak. Many years ago when we first played this venue, we were shown into the reptile house and were told on this occasion that would be our changing room.

It turns out that the reptile house at Toledo Zoo is one of only a few dedicated reptile houses in the world, exhibiting species such as the Aruba Island Rattlesnake and many turtles, lizards, snakes and spiders of varying sizes, hairiness and scariness. This has to be the most unusual dressing room I have ever been offered. Getting ready to walk on stage to be observed at close quarters by thousands of people brought about a whole new level of empathy with these creatures. And as I was using the reflection of the window to the lizard's quarters to check my clothes, we had a moment together, this lizard and I, and I swear he gave me a look that said, 'I know exactly how you feel, buddy.'

As the show started early on this night (7.30pm) and we were at the height of summer, the majority of the concert was played in broad daylight. It's a different atmosphere for both the band and audience, as each can see the whites of the other's eyes. I don't have a preference either way, although I have to say it's great to be able to see the expressions on people's faces as the show progresses. Incidentally, when we travel, we tour with our own stage carpet, the amount of which would easily decorate a small family home.

It's used for two reasons: firstly, it has markings on it to ensure all the gear set on top of it is in the same place each night – drum kits, microphone stands, keyboards etc. And secondly, it creates a familiar and comfortable surface to walk on, as opposed to the often inconsistent floorings of the venues.

The last time we played at the zoo, the weather conditions offered nothing less than torrential rain, necessitating the leaving behind of the carpet. What appeared to be about 1,000 gallons of rainwater descended on us before, during and after our performance, so much in fact that the crew was physically unable to lift the combined weight of carpet and rainwater. So they simply left it in place, and bought another one from Carpets 'R' Us or somewhere similar the following day. Thankfully last night's show was conducted in glorious sunshine, with the warm summer evening heat that makes concerts like this an utter pleasure.

Yesterday's travel is what we call a 'hit and run.' We set off from Cleveland due west along the southern part of Lake Erie, on the 150-mile journey to Toledo at 1.00 in the afternoon. Both the 2010 World Cup quarterfinals and the Wimbledon men's semi-final of Andy Murray v Rafael Nadal were playing on the in-bus entertainment system. With John being such a keen tennis player we watched Wimbledon. The return journey started shortly after the concert, and we all arrived back in the early hours of the morning to Cleveland where we play tonight.

**Postcard 21**

FOR CORRESPONDENCE   FOR ADDRESS ONLY

Saturday
July 3rd
2010

Nautica Pavilion,
Cleveland, Ohio,
USA

Serie Nº 714 S.B.

The Rock 'n' Roll Hall of Fame has a long list of esteemed inductees, ranging from U2 to the Hollies, the Supremes to Les Paul. For some reason, at the time of writing in July 2010, the widely acclaimed and legendary rock band The Moody Blues – who have sold over 70 million albums, had countless hit records, and were part of the original British Invasion of rock music to the US in the 1960s – is not one of them. This has caused collective scratching of heads from the band, record executives, managers and fans alike. It simply doesn't make sense; three of the five original band members still tour all over the world to sellout (and very appreciative) audiences in major venues. And in addition to that, I've been playing with them for the past 20 years! Go figure, as our American friends would say.

The above notwithstanding, Cleveland has always been a hugely successful and popular place for this band to play. The concert at the Nautica Pavilion located in The Flats in downtown Cleveland beside the Cuyahoga River proved to be no different. In previous years we have played at the Blossom Music Centre, and on several occasions performed with the Cleveland Orchestra. Cleveland sits on the southern shore of Lake Erie, with the Cuyahoga River running though it, and if I were to take a long enough run I could jump from the drum riser into the river, so close is the stage to the water.

There was a masseuse backstage, with a table set outside in the sun on the decking next to the water, behind flowing Bedouin-style curtains – a perfect setting. I quickly put my name down for a session before the show with Missy, an athletic young girl who looked about 12 years of age to me. However, once she started work, it became clear she would easily beat Mike Tyson at arm wrestling. My suffering shoulders, which were feeling stiff from a combination of flailing arms and typing on my computer while being propped up by pillows in my bunk, were treated to 30 minutes of utter bliss. Deep tissue massage is a must on these tours from time to time.

The Pavilion is positioned on a bend of the Cuyahoga River known as Collision Bend, and as I sat on stage the river sort of wrapped around from behind, so even a cursory glance left or right brought into view the snakelike route of the river from each side, even though my back was to it when sitting at the drums. It gave the feeling of being out on a precipice.

The Pavilion is itself attached to an old rusted swing bridge, which sticks up into the air like a see-through tower block leaning slightly out over the river, so much so I think they should rename it the Leaning Tower of Cleveland. This early crossing, which hasn't been used in over 70 years, used to be winched down over the river to allow steam trains to cross, after which it was winched back up into its current position. It remains there as an elegant, rusting monument to a more industrial and romantic yesteryear. In comparison to the other more modern structures surrounding our pinnacle at the concert stand, it strikes a dramatic pose.

In both directions following the river there are bridges in working condition, one of which is a small suspension bridge. In fact, so populated is this area with postindustrial remnants that there are ·

bridges over bridges. As the bigger boats approach Collision Bend, they slow down and sound a very loud horn in order to prompt the suspension bridge operators — who are just out of view from the drum stool — to begin their work of raising the newer working bridge to allow the larger vessels through. As boats pass quite often, it is not out of the ordinary to have something resembling a small QE2 let off a deafening five-second blast of hot air from an onboard giant tuba.

During the soundcheck — and also the performance — boats of all shapes and sizes pulled up behind the stage, and we acquired a second, non-paying, audience. It was fun turning around at times to take a bow to the floating spectators.

As our show progressed, one of the larger boats approached Collision Bend during a rather up-tempo piece with an energetic beat. *(I'm Just) a Singer in a Rock 'n' Roll Band* is probably the rockiest song of the set. It always gets the crowd on their feet, and is more often than not a showstopper. I didn't see, but I found out later the passengers came to the side of the boat to watch the show as the vessel slowed. The captain waited until we finished the song and then pulled down on a rope to sound the horn. Along with thousands of applauding fans in both The Pavilion and on the vessel, he let off an almighty boat belch. If I didn't know he was behind me before, I certainly knew after his impromptu announcement.

Some time ago we played at The Blossom Music Centre, a bigger arena than The Pavilion with a rabbit warren of backstage corridors. On this occasion The Moody Blues had a support band that were newly signed and at the beginning of their career — they were young and were very hip indeed, with ripped jeans and leather jackets and they looked for the entire world like a group of serious rockers.

Supermodel-type girls always surrounded them – the whole troupe resembled something you would see on the front cover of Vogue magazine.

As The Moody Blues were headlining, we would go on last, and the hip underlings would be backstage in their dressing room already partying with their entourage. On one particular night, The Moodies finished the set with the usual wonderful standing ovation, to cheers of 10,000 or so fans. I was first off stage followed by the whole band, all walking in single file behind me down the stairs at the side of the stage, where we began winding our way to our quarters.

We were laughing and joking, talking and shouting back to one another, and generally still in the moment of adulation, somewhat unaware of our surroundings. As I traipsed towards our dressing rooms, with the others close behind, I glanced at the support act sitting down on couches with their girlfriends, drinking and smoking. As my conga line walked past them, I could have sworn they were staring with a look of admiration. It turned out to be a look of total confusion – we walked past them into the cul-de-sac of their communal showers in their dressing room, having become completely lost after leaving the stage. Rock 'n' roll Cleveland.

**Postcard 22**

FOR CORRESPONDENCE     FOR ADDRESS ONLY

Sunday
July 4th
2010

Hamilton, Ontario,
Canada

Serie N° 714 H.S.

Yesterday we left Cleveland on The Good Ship Everything around 11.00am to drive 260 miles to Hamilton, Ontario, in Canada. The next five days of our tour will be conducted in Canada.

To leave America we began the journey by travelling east along Route 90 on the south side of Lake Erie, passing through the town of Erie but not stopping, in the direction of Buffalo, New York on the Canadian border. The American/Canadian border travels up the centre of Lake Erie, to the west of Buffalo carrying on up river to Niagara Falls, and then the border continues along the water, up to Lake Ontario, which feeds Niagara Falls.

As the tour bus approached the border crossing, I noticed an inordinate number of vehicles attempting to leave America, which I thought an unusual phenomenon, today of all days. When we got near the border it became clear we were going to be pushing it to make the gig on time with all this traffic. David, our bus driver, managed to get us out of trouble by using a wonderful trick for getting to the front of the line. He simply drove past everyone and pulled into an empty bay reserved for official vehicles. A border security officer came over to tell him he couldn't park there, and David beautifully feigned ignorance.

'Oh, sorry buddy, do you want me to back up?'

The officer took one look at the length of the bus, and obviously calculated it would be near impossible to back a vehicle of this size back down the line and said, 'Oh forget it, you're here now.' So the paperwork for the whole group was concluded quickly and at around 4.00pm we pulled into Hamilton. Our venue for the first of two nights was the Hamilton Place Theatre, which holds about 3,000 people. As we got off the bus I swear I heard David say, 'Works every time,' but I don't know what he was talking about... Although we were playing two concerts, we were essentially here for just one day. We had to check out of the hotel room in the afternoon of day two, before the second show, because after that show we were driving overnight to Montréal.

Hamilton was one of those communities I found easy to snub on first viewing. In comparison to many other places we've visited, it didn't appear to have a lot going for it. The shops immediately surrounding the theatre and hotel opposite were not that inspiring. However, I was mistaken. The city is a port situated on the southwest tip of Lake Ontario just 42 miles west of Niagara Falls. It's essentially right smack bang in the middle of the Great Lakes, and as a consequence is surrounded by breathtaking views. Given more time it would surely offer many more surprises.

The morning saw me attempting one of my exploratory jaunts on foot in the direction of the Lake which, I could see from my hotel window, was about 12 blocks away. It was, however, so incredibly hot that I only managed a distance of two blocks before concluding it would be positively suicidal if I ventured further. Under the dome of the blue sky I felt like a soldier ant caught on the concrete surface of a school playground. As I ran forward – or should I say jogged slowly

– in the direction of my nose, it was as if I was running through a set of velvet curtains in a sauna: it was the type of heat you feel when you open the dishwasher too soon after the cycle and you get a face full of hot steam.

So I abandoned this foolish enterprise rather quickly and returned to the comfort of my air-conditioned room, by way of the hotel gym. Although the gym was air-conditioned, it too was exceedingly hot. Justin and Norda were in there, and I sweated more in the short workout than I do during a concert.

Arriving back in my room after the workout at around 2.00pm, I was faced with the frequent challenge of having some very wet clothes to pack. So I will offer you today a well-known in-room laundry trick. All that is required is a large towel, some hotel shampoo and a pair of Nike running shoes.

I realised after getting back to the room that I had only 90 minutes to wash - and more importantly, dry - my running gear as much as possible before packing it in a case. I set about this familiar chore with conviction. Stripping off the items that need washing, I am left, albeit in the privacy of my hotel room wearing nothing but a pair of Nike running shoes – one of the shoes still dark from its mud bath in Chicago. Although it's as clean as it's going to get, it has a slight terracotta look to it - quite different to its twin brother on my left foot.

I placed the shirt and shorts in the sink with the entire contents of the miniature shampoo bottle, and running the hot tap I vigorously washed through the items as much as possible by hand. Once I had rinsed them through, I laid out a hotel towel flat on the floor and then placed the items flat on top of the towel, and then very carefully rolled the wet clothes into it.

This activity can be made more pleasant if you have an iPod shuffle and listen to some Earth, Wind and Fire, even if the item is swinging around as it hangs from your ears; it adds tempo to the enterprise. While Maurice White is singing falsetto, you place your feet as wide apart as possible and take one end of the rolled up bath towel and put it under your left foot (the reason I keep my running shoes on is to get a better grip of the towel at one end). Then twist the other end around as much as you can, and pull. This squeezes out all the moisture from the clothes into the towel.

Apparently 'Do not disturb' signs hanging on hotel door handles do not count for much in Canada. The maid walked into my room as if she were entering the front door to an empty house. It wasn't my fault I didn't hear her; I was wearing an iPod, after all. This type of laundering is a perfectly normal and everyday occurrence to me; it really didn't dawn on me what this activity may look like when viewed by another. The sight of a naked man wearing running shoes, apparently attempting to strangle a hotel bath towel, clearly took her by surprise. Maurice stopped singing just in time for me to hear her scream 'Furjeezuscrissake' and fall backwards out of the door, before I could offer a succinct explanation.

She allowed it to slam rather loudly as she let go of the handle, just to add some rather unnecessary drama to the unfortunate ceremony, I thought. By the time I had put a robe on and peeped through that little hole in the door – you know, the one that makes you feel like a one-eyed fish looking out of a bowl - she was nowhere to be seen. I packed, and looking rather suspicious I'm sure, crept from the room to check out, hoping not to (and thankfully I didn't) see a maid on the way.

## Postcard 23

FOR CORRESPONDENCE    FOR ADDRESS ONLY

Monday
July 5th
2010

Hamilton, Ontario,
Canada
to
Montréal, Québec,
Canada

Serie Nº 714 N.S.

The shows in Hamilton were simply great. On the occasions when we do two concerts in the same venue, there can be a tendency to compare, but as a lot of the audience was there both nights, we had an absolutely tremendous reception. It's wonderful to be a part of this touring experience, but I can only imagine what it must be like to have written this material, and decades later to be standing on stage having it applauded.

The music of The Moody Blues really has become a major part in the lives of many, and clearly still triggers emotions in lots of people. One of the many effects of music, when it enters our lives at the same time as important events (births, deaths, marriages, etc.), is that it becomes connected to the magnitude of the emotion. When we hear those melodies later in life, they stimulate deeply held emotions, and the music takes on an unexpected significance. So I am not at all surprised when I see people in the audience with tears of emotion listening to the very people who created the music. Performing music is one thing, creating it is another thing altogether, doing both is sublime.

I successfully checked out of the hotel at 4.00pm yesterday, after the maid happened upon me in all my sartorial elegance during my laundry session. The rest of the day was spent backstage filling the hours approaching the performance with a combination of some light reading and a power nap.

After the second show in Hamilton, The Good Ship Everything – with our trusty driver, David – was all set for the overnight 400-mile trek to Montreal. This journey takes about eight hours by bus, but on this occasion we first dropped the three principal guys off at the airport, as they took a small Lear jet that got them to Montreal in about an hour and a half. In the meantime, we backing musicians were left to slum it on a multi-million dollar tour bus, with a fridge full of food, a bar full of booze, several large flat screen TVs and eight comfortable bunks to choose from. To quote a colleague, 'This job does not suck.'

Changing into pyjamas is a delicate affair on a moving tour bus that houses mixed genders. Thankfully we can cordon off the central bunk area with electric sliding doors that have a swooshing sound effect right out of *Star Trek*. We take it in turns to undergo the metamorphosis from rock band to slumber party. I managed to avoid the temptation of streaking down the bus for shock value, as one never knows how these things will be taken. It may be a rock 'n' roll tour, but I have to remind myself that we are, after all, professionals in our 50s (some of us) and not a teenage pop band. Thankfully the urge passed in a millisecond.

Once settled in my bunk, I experienced a small feeling of euphoria as I plumped up the pillows. With all needs taken care of and all decisions made for me – travel, food, destination, etc. – I allowed myself a few moments of reflection on what it is I do: halfway through a rock 'n' roll tour in America with a famous band, having my creative talents applauded every night, the respect of my peers, money going into the bank in the UK, and a daily amount of cash for expenses brings on an exhilarating micro-moment of all-encompassing pleasure.

As I positioned myself on my left side, with pillows tucked from head to toe both behind me and in front of me (for stability), my mind wandered to my family. My wife and two children are back in the UK, and this is the second of four tours this year; I haven't seen them for over two weeks and I won't be seeing them for a further two weeks. I began reflecting on all the birthdays missed; my daughters' end-of-term plays performed in my absence; wedding anniversaries celebrated with a phone call; entire summer holidays passing by without me being there... the list goes on.

Within seconds my emotional balloon of jubilation began deflating at an alarming rate. My earlier moment of happiness disappeared quickly and was replaced by a deep feeling of melancholy. There is a very heavy price to pay indeed for such a life. I fell to sleep quickly in my berth, with mixed emotions.

The Good Ship Everything pulled into Montreal at 6.30am. I remained asleep for the entire journey, and managed to negotiate the short distance from bunk to hotel bed with familiar lethargic ease. After I had phoned home in an attempt to ease my guilty conscience for not being there, I climbed into a bed that felt like a cloud in comparison to the bunk, and slept until 11.00am.

**Postcard 24**

FOR CORRESPONDENCE · FOR ADDRESS ONLY

Tuesday
July 6th
2010

Salle Wilfrid Pelletier
Theatre, Montreal,
Québec,
Canada

Serie N° 114 4 5

Montreal, Quebec (originally known as Ville-Marie or 'City of Mary' but now pronounced 'Keybeck' by the locals) is an amazing place. With street names like Place Jean Paul Riopelle, Rue de Bleury, and Rue Saint Jacques, we might as well be in Europe. This francophone city is the second largest primarily French-speaking city in the world, after Paris. And I find many occupants (mostly taxi drivers) either refuse to, or can't, speak English. The city is vibrating with an unusual heat at the time of this writing, which adds another dimension to the experience. Walking around the European-looking buildings and streets of the old town is reminiscent of family holidays in France – the wonderful aromas of bistros bring back memories. We are here to play on the final day of the Montréal Jazz Festival.

As it was too hot (again) to run anywhere, yesterday I walked through the old town to the port on the St Laurence River that connects the Great Lakes to the Atlantic Ocean. There is a small peninsula that sticks out to the north like a finger into the water. The road that runs the length of the finger, which becomes a bridge spanning the river, is the Avenue Pierre Dupuy, which can clearly be observed from the port. This position offers a view of one of the most unusual buildings I think I have ever seen, called Habitat 67. It looks like an architectural mistake. If a four-year-old erected a toy building with some cardboard boxes, letting their imagination dictate shape and design with no consideration for stability or structure, they would be left with something that resembles Habitat 67. It looks like a sturdy wind would blow it over. In fact it was created for Montreal's 'Expo 67', one of the world's largest universal expositions. It is an amazing piece of architecture.

While I was standing at the water's edge trying to decide if I liked it or not, I couldn't help but notice a giant refinery and old flour mill close to it, which was a leftover from the industrial age and not at all attractive. So looking for something a little more pleasing to the eye, I walked north along Rue de la Commune Quest, by the water's edge, in the direction of the Notre Dame Basilica (a church). Strolling in the baking sun, following the hotel map, I managed to successfully plot a course through the decidedly French-looking streets to my destination. On the way I was treated to a beautiful fountain here, a statue over there – all of which gave it a splash of French authenticity.

By the time I arrived at the church I was drenched through with perspiration (definitely a good job I wasn't running) and wanted somewhere cool to escape from the heat. I was hoping for something comfortable, old-fashioned and quietly grand in this Notre Dame, not at all expecting it to compare with the 'real thing' in Paris.

When I walked into the building, it took my breath away. Notre Dame Basilica had a magnificent interior, as grandiose and majestic as anything I have ever seen. This house of God can hold thousands of worshippers, and its gothic revival architecture is considered among the most dramatic in the world. I spent two hours in there just looking in wonder at what humans can create when they put their minds to it.

**Later...**

Our concert was at the Salle Wiffrid Pelletier Theatre, with a full capacity audience of 3,000. Built in 1963 by Dimitri Dimakoloulos and Fred Lebensold, it had a modern but intimate atmosphere to it. As soon as we started to play the 90-minute straight-through set, I knew it was going to be good. I looked over to Alan Hewitt on keyboards, and his facial expression showed that he was feeling exactly the same.

Audiences are different all over the world; some are more reserved than others. For instance, in some parts of India, they don't clap, they just hum loudly in appreciation. Americans, in my opinion, tend to be the most enthusiastic. Although Canadian audiences are generally considered to be a little more reserved, they certainly didn't behave that way at this gig.

As a group we are settled into this tour now, and the music is seriously tight, energetic and confident in performance. The listeners must pick up on these elements, as the reception was completely overwhelming, with show stopping applause after only the fourth number. At the end of the show, when I went through to have a glass of wine with Justin in the tuning room, we both agreed it was one of the best of the tour.

Some people listen to the shipping forecast on the radio for amusement, or so I am told. I amuse myself by reading the Economist magazine and all the newspapers I can get my hands on. However, since I started writing this book and reading a series of autobiographies, I simply have not had the time nor the inclination to follow the news. As a consequence I am completely ignorant of world events since leaving home three weeks ago. It was as much as I could do to keep abreast of the 2010 World Cup and Wimbledon tennis competitions. I haven't switched a single hotel television on at any point on the tour. And the discovery that the world keeps turning without me hanging on to the latest news bulletin is refreshing indeed. I might be on to something here.

**Postcard 25**

FOR CORRESPONDENCE

FOR ADDRESS ONLY

Wednesday
July 7th
2010

Montreal, Quebec,
Canada

Serie N° 7144 8

Enjoying a day off in a place like Montreal is a rare treat indeed, even when there is a heatwave. The only hindrance was that, inexplicably, none of us were able to access emails while being here, which meant that when we got to somewhere with working Wi-Fi, there would be hundreds of messages eagerly awaiting consideration from everybody on this tour.

As the heat wave continued, I found I only had the energy to leisurely tread once more in the steps of the previous day, trying to find little nuggets of interest. However, my timing was out of kilter. One of the side effects of touring is the inevitable consequence of the working day being back to front. On a normal day in the UK, I wake in the morning enjoying an early breakfast before getting to work in my studio. The latest I would get to bed at home would be around midnight, and I like to be up with my wife early enough to wake the kids for school.

On tour, I arrive in my 'office' around 8.00pm when the show starts. The working day is therefore somewhat turned around. This is the most important part of the day, and let's face it – it is the reason I'm here. Everything leading up to the performance is geared to being ready for that single event. When we travel after a show and arrive late at a hotel, it often requires sleeping until late morning in order to have enough rest to function the following day. It's not unusual to get to sleep at 2.00am or often much later, and if there have been a series of back-to-back gigs, the day off becomes more a recovery day than anything else. Today, however, proved a little more interesting.

I managed to ask the concierge (from the phone next to the bed while I was still in it) for recreational options later in the day and was told there was a classical concert at the Notre Dame Basilica at 6.30pm. This is where I decided the evening was going to start. First, though, I had to get out of bed, and at 11.00am I was finding it difficult to raise any enthusiasm for the concept. Hunger was the final motivation, and I gingerly arose, my body communicating to me the downside of sleeping on a tour bus and pounding a drum kit.

A most enjoyable and relaxing morning ensued, with me settling into a comfy chair in the shade outside a café with a coffee and a rather delicious toasted mozzarella sandwich, which I had to pretend was breakfast. Of course by the time I began to eat food at midday, the morning had officially ended, which meant I was faced with just an afternoon/evening off instead of a full day. Nevertheless, my body was thanking me for not forcing it around to more sights, and allowing it to gently rest in the warmth. A happy two hours' reading passed, during which John walked by and joined me for a coffee for 10 minutes.

By 4.00pm I was ready for lunch, or early dinner, or whatever the afternoon equivalent of brunch is. So I ambled very leisurely along the road just a couple of blocks from the hotel to a little restaurant-cum-bistro called Holder. It was a typically French establishment, with dark wooden tables, paper tablecloths over heavy linen, and the sort of décor that suggests class without pretentiousness. Moules marinière accompanied by glass of chilled Pinot Grigio was a fine choice indeed.

The concert at the church was something I was really looking forward to – I was hoping to hear the church organ in all its glory. My Uncle Peter used to be the organist and choirmaster at St Paul's Cathedral in London, and I have sweet childhood memories of the magnificent sound of him playing a church organ. I arrived at the Notre Dame Basilica 15 minutes before the concert, payed ten Canadian dollars for the ticket and joined the line filing into the church. It was still sweltering hot.

Imagine my disappointment as I walked through the main doors and was given a really old-fashioned iPod-looking device with a set of even older headphones. I'm used to in-ear monitors, for goodness' sake. As I walked to the pew to take my seat, I saw the entire church had been covered in white screens, and my disgruntlement was complete when a 30-minute film of the history of the church – performed by the worst type of soap-opera actors, with the sound coming through the headphones – ensued.

Pause with me for a moment while we put this scenario into perspective. Here we have a magnificent church organ listed as one of the world's largest, with 7,000 pipes, in a church of breathtaking architectural beauty. When you arrive for a concert, you are presented with a screen-covered church, a set of dodgy headphones, and the most pitiful attempt at entertainment that you can imagine! Doesn't make much sense, what?

The evening wasn't a complete disaster, as I did manage to find a place afterwards, just a few blocks away from the hotel, with a lovely little jazz trio playing (it should have been a quartet but the drummer didn't turn up). A tuna salad and a polite glass of rosé was all I needed to turn the day around. After my culturally alternative supper, I collapsed into bed at midnight.

**Postcard 26**

FOR CORRESPONDENCE

FOR ADDRESS ONLY

*Thursday*
*July 8th*
*2010*

*Montreal, Quebec, Canada*
*to*
*Ottawa Bluesfest, Ottawa,*
*Ontario, Canada*
*to*
*Rochester, New York,*
*USA*

Serie Nº 7/14-6-5

Today it was brought to my attention that I'm not fully aware of where we're going. I awoke this morning quite happily looking forward to traveling to Quebec City, only to check the itinerary to realise we were actually going in completely the opposite direction; Ottawa, the capital of Canada. Oh well, it's an interesting life.

The day was to encompass three cities, two countries, and 'overnighting' the final border crossing on The Good Ship Everything to the end destination, which if I am not mistaken is back in America somewhere.

The morning began with a very late breakfast sitting outside a café next to the hotel, letting the time pass at a leisurely pace with a good book. Opposite my reading quarters was a small park with fountains, which came into their own on this day of bright blue sky and simmering heat.

About an hour before lobby call for the drive to Ottawa, I heard percussion sounds emanating from the park, rather like a drummer warming up. The jazz festival was officially over, so I wasn't expecting to hear amplified sounds outdoors today. Of course the prospect of listening to local musicians play in any setting will get me out of whatever seat I happen to be occupying. So, I wandered in the direction of the sounds.

On closer inspection I saw a small stage, with a few acoustic guitars, and some very dark, handsome, and exotic-looking musicians setting up – I think perhaps they were Spanish. The drummer was playing a rhythm for a soundcheck (in a very small and intimate setting) on a kit setup I've never seen before. The bass drum was in the right place, but instead of the snare drum that would normally sit between the drummer's legs (allowing his right foot to operate the bass drum pedal) was a djembe. This is a skin-covered hand-drum, shaped like a large goblet and played with bare hands. In place of his stool, there was a cajón (pronounced ka-hon...), which is a kind of box drum that you sit on, and play between your legs by slapping different parts of it to get different tones. The centre has a deeper sound, and from the outer sides, which contain metal, comes a high percussive tone when hit. When played properly it's a very sophisticated instrument indeed. And this guy could play.

Of course I introduced myself when they finished the sound check, as I wanted to know when they were going to play properly. I was in luck, as they were about to begin, and after a very interesting chat with the drummer they set about playing Flamenco, the likes of which I don't think I had ever heard before. With the drummer's modern approach, in addition to his serious Latin chops, he created a magnificent texture of rhythms, which resembled an all-out percussion section. He did tell me his name, but it sounded like Manuel Bosnia and Herzegovina, and after the second attempt it seemed rude to ask a third time, so I left it at that. I enjoyed 20 minutes of wonderful music before dawdling back to the hotel only 200 feet away, to join the bus for the journey to the Canadian capital.

We drove 130 miles during the day, arriving at 6.00pm. The Ottawa

Bluesfest was well underway, with three huge stages, a collection of stalls and tents, and tens of thousands of people milling around. As with the Summerfest in Cleveland we arrived on The Good Ship Everything behind our stage as another band was playing. They were very good indeed, although I still don't know who they were. Once more, a trailer played the part of a dressing room – thankfully with excellent air conditioning as the heatwave progressed. I had sympathy for the crew who had been erecting the equipment in direct sunlight the entire day.

Using my laminated 'Access All Areas' pass, I walked out into the fair to have a look around. I checked out all the stalls and walked the several hundred yards between each of the three stages. Every hour a band started playing on a different stage, meaning music was playing somewhere all the time. The hour before we played, the Bacon Brothers Band were playing on an adjacent stage. The lead singer was Kevin Bacon, the Hollywood actor, he and his brother both sang and played guitars. They were playing away looking and sounding every bit like a true rock band. We were due to go on our stage at 8.00pm, with the B-52s following us at 9.30pm on yet another stage.

After deciding the gig in Montreal was probably one of the best this tour, I have to say this outdoor music festival in Ottawa topped even that. Playing outdoors on a purpose-built stage to tens of thousands of people at the height of summer is what you would call living the dream. The audience increased in size as our 90-minute set progressed. The band was introduced as 'legendary', so it felt like the audience was standing there waiting to see what we had to offer. Playing with the combined assurance of the previous gigs of the tour, we launched confidently into the set. It started out wonderfully, and ended on a high that you only get from playing to so many people.

Although I didn't see him, somebody told me that Kevin Bacon and his band came and stood at the side of the stage for about four numbers. Justin mentioned it on the tour bus afterwards, and I felt almost ridiculously pleased at the news. It's not every day a Hollywood star comes to check out a performance that I'm involved in.

Our overnight journey was not one of the easiest, as the road was tediously bumpy, and I for one was constantly being woken as the night advanced. We arrived at an anonymous hotel somewhere around 4.00am. I climbed into an unfamiliar bed and slumbered fitfully until 10.00am. As my eyes opened I spoke the on-tour-musician's-mantra out loud to an empty hotel room. 'Where the hell am I?' Does this constitute talking to myself?

## Postcard 27

FOR CORRESPONDENCE   FOR ADDRESS ONLY

Friday
July 9th
2010

Rochester, New York,
USA
to
Canandaigua, New York,
USA
(and back again)

With the words 'Where the hell am I?' still ringing in my ears at 10am this morning, I dragged myself out of bed. While gathering my senses I looked at the address printed in miniature on my hotel telephone, which informed me I was in Rochester, New York. You know you are on a rock 'n' roll tour when you wake up and don't know where you are, but it's also a little disconcerting standing there gazing out of the window with a blank look, wondering which day it is. I decided I needed to study the itinerary for 15 minutes just to establish that I was not living in some parallel universe.

The itinerary told me it was Friday July 9th, I was staying in Rochester, New York, but would be playing tonight in Canandaigua, New York, about 30 miles away. After the concert we come back to this hotel, and tomorrow we drive to Bethel Woods for a show at the original site of Woodstock. Got that? Good. Thank heavens for the Book of Lies, as today it validated my sanity.

The next challenge was to establish exactly which neighbourhood I was in, and where to get breakfast. The view from my hotel room told me a great deal. I could see one burned out building, which had clearly been in that condition for some time, and the top of an empty multi-storey car park. The only other visible area was a restricted view of the road with one shop called Family Dollar. This retail establishment didn't look very salubrious, to say the least, and the kindest I can be in my observation of this neighbourhood was that it was not very well-heeled. I was obviously looking down on the side of the track that made the other side look good.

I've lived in neighbourhoods like this in the UK, and when you know the area and the people, normally there is nothing to worry about. But when you're a stranger, it's a whole different ball game. Thinking of myself as a streetwise kind of guy and having travelled and visited all sorts of places, I'm still surprised at the sort of decisions I find myself making when going out into these types of neighbourhoods. For instance, I removed my watch, bracelet and silver necklace and wore a dark pair of shorts and an old T-shirt. Walking out into the street and contemplating my surroundings, I congratulated myself on what appeared to be some wise sartorial decision-making. Although we had stayed here many years ago, the area had since adopted a remarkably unsavoury tone.

Holding a book with the hotel map concealed inside, I walked in the direction of the local café chosen from Google, with as much momentum as I could muster. Being forced to stop at the first junction and to wait on the sidewalk to cross the road was a deeply disturbing experience; as around me lay a group of teenagers in a very unorganised fashion, wearing bandanas on their heads and their jeans around their knees. I'm sure they were not interested in me, but as I dared not look at them I couldn't determine the fact either way.

I decided to jaywalk across the street just to prove I was a devil-may-care individual, and to get away from the junction as quickly as possible. Having seen how low the local residents' trousers were slung, I was slightly comforted by the Confucius quotation: 'Woman with dress around waist can run faster than man with trousers round ankles.' This may not be entirely precise, but you get the gist.

After only a few minutes, this little walk had got my heart racing, and I wasn't even jogging. Arriving at the next junction and initially being pleased that the illuminated white flashing man ushered me to cross the road, I noticed a very large, elderly lady in a motorised wheelchair crossing on the opposite road to my left. She was wearing a pair of dark sunglasses, and as my side of the road had a go signal for pedestrians, I presumed her side must have had a stop signal. In the seconds it took me to process this information, a car crossed the junction and hit the corner of her wheelchair spinning her 90° to the left.

Thankfully, as I ran to the lady in the wheelchair to help her, the car pulled over. The vehicle had struck her leg at about 20 miles an hour, but as I knelt down next to her to take a look, I couldn't see any damage to her or the wheelchair. And to be truthful she had such a thick southern accent and was slurring her words so much I was having difficulty communicating with her, although I did manage to get the name Doris from her.

I tried to get Doris off the road and onto the sidewalk by moving the little joystick on the electric wheelchair, but not having operated one of these chariots before, the two of us weaved left and right, uncomfortably working our way off the road like a wounded animal. The whole event would have been comical if it were not so serious. The car reversed back to the scene of the incident, but instead of the driver getting out he just wound the window down and looked at me. 'You better get out, you've just hit this lady in a wheelchair with your car,' I said automatically.

By now Doris was complaining that her right leg was hurting. However, although the car had hit her at speed and spun her around, it was clear she was in a bad way before this accident. Whatever had happened to Doris before, this was still the luckiest day of her life. Had she been a few inches further on, this would've been a very different story.

Looking rather concerned, the young driver (probably in his 20s) got out of the car, although I feared he was more worried about himself than the welfare of Doris. He had long black curly hair, which stuck out at random angles from a colourful bandana, some very thick gold chains around his neck, and multiple pairs of shorts; the top layer – jeans – starting at his knees, then a pair of boxer shorts exposed in their entirety, then another pair of briefs sticking out the top of the boxer shorts. The other noticeable characteristic was the sheer amount of tattoos covering any exposed skin. Considering his whereabouts and demeanor, I began to have a sinking feeling he was what we might call a gang member. Within a few short sentences it was obvious he was also a couple of sandwiches short of a picnic. Although I asked, I have absolutely no idea what his name was, as it was spoken through lips that didn't move and had far too many syllables for me to remember, so I'll refer to him as Kevin.

Since Doris clearly had to be seen by a doctor and I didn't

have my phone with me I barked at Kevin 'Call an ambulance.'
Kevin asked, 'What's the number?'

With a look of incredulity I'm sure, I replied, 'Er... well... I'm not from these parts, but why don't you try 911?'

When Kevin got through he handed me the phone, as he was incapable of venturing any meaningful information to the emergency services. So, I found myself laying out the hotel map on the sidewalk at the scene of the accident, and talking to 911 on a possible gang member's phone, trying to work out and describe where we were, and what happened.

I am not exaggerating when I say in less than three minutes and with sirens blazing, a fire engine, an ambulance, two police cars and five policemen on bicycles arrived at the scene. These guys had the whole process down to a fine art and were obviously used to these adventures. Thankfully this story calms down a bit from here, as Doris appeared to be relatively OK, and Kevin mercifully had a driving license and was apparently legal.

As I didn't want Kevin to get into any unnecessary trouble I tried to point out to an American policeman in a slightly hyperventilated voice, but with my best English accent that 'It really wasn't this gentleman's fault, the lady in the wheelchair was crossing on a red light, and he immediately came back to help,' which was of course true. The look on Kevin's face at these words was one of complete gratitude. I spoke these words for the added insurance of not being a potential victim of a drive-by shooting just around the corner – although I'm probably doing Kevin a complete disservice in this assumption. It's amazing what the mind concludes in high stress situations.

Doris was carefully lifted into an ambulance by five men and taken to hospital, Kevin was allowed to leave, and I continued on for my breakfast, which I did not at all enjoy.

At the concert that evening, it was agreed that maybe this hotel should be removed from the list for a while. So while affairs in this neighbourhood are probably not as bad as I have described, I doubt we'll be here again any time soon. Tomorrow is another hit and run gig (no pun intended), but on this occasion I know exactly where we're going. Goodnight.

**Postcard 28**

FOR CORRESPONDENCE     FOR ADDRESS ONLY

Saturday
July 10th
2010

Bethel, New York,
USA
to
Woodstock, New York,
USA

If an alchemist were ever able to bottle and sell the post-gig emotion of exultation, they would make a fortune, as I know of no other feeling quite like it. It's a combination of excitement, exhilaration and jubilation with a little triumph thrown in for good measure. These are not emotions you will hear being expressed often at a place of work, but there you are.

Tonight's concert was at the Bethel Woods Centre for the Performing Arts, which is the site of the original 1969 Woodstock Festival – one of music's most legendary venues.

In order to arrive at this high, however, we first have to leave the scene of the previous day's activities. My night's sleep back in Rochester, NY was interrupted with several emergency-service sirens passing the hotel during the night. Unlike in the UK, here I'm unable to tell the difference, so it could have been any of my friends from the preceding day's incident – fire engine, ambulance or police – take your pick. On personal safety grounds, I decided to give breakfast in yesterday's little café a miss, and instead revisited my in-room breakfast recipe – with a twist. This time it was a full protein drink blended with water, porridge oats, and yogurt, meaning I checked out of the hotel feeling conclusively full but without incurring an 'extras' bill.

We were once again aboard The Good Ship Everything at midday for a four and a half-hour journey to Bethel Woods, New York. These long bus journeys during the day tend to pass quite painlessly through a combination of humourous band interaction, political debate (normally conducted at the back of the bus between Graeme and myself), and some extended measures of zoning out. A stint at the front of the bus chatting with David our driver and watching the scenery pass by is also a great way to dispatch a few hours.

Arriving at Bethel Woods, it became immediately clear someone had gone to a great deal of effort to erect one of the most beautiful amphitheatres I think I have ever seen. This venue, which began in its current form in 1996, has become a premier cultural destination for concertgoers and music lovers by providing not only a simply fabulous performance facility, but also a museum dedicated to the legacy of the Woodstock Festival, and all the topics (political and social), which the event represented.

Although a great deal has been written about the Woodstock Festival, I can tell you, now I've visited the museum, that it was originally billed as an Aquarian Exposition: Three days of peace and music near a hamlet called White Lake in the town of Bethel, New York. At the time the site was owned by Max Yasgur, a dairy farmer.

The festival spanned the three days from August 15th to 18th 1969. Thirty-two acts performed outdoors to an audience of half a million. It is well known to be one of the most pivotal moments in popular music history, and is listed in *Rolling Stone* Magazine as one of the top 50 moments that changed the history of rock 'n' roll. The photographs and multi-media presentations in the museum show a relaxed, chaotic gathering of people, with the emphasis on peace and political change – doing anything they wanted. They really were exploring the outer boundaries of what was considered socially acceptable at the time.

Among the artists performing on Friday August 15th – the first day of the 1969 festival – were Ravi Shankar and Joan Baez. On Saturday August 16th, Santana, Canned Heat, the Grateful Dead, Creedence Clearwater Revival, Janis Joplin, Sly and the Family Stone, The Who, and Jefferson Airplane were just some of the artists performing. It ended with Joe Cocker, Blood Sweat and Tears, Crosby, Stills, Nash and Young, and Jimi Hendrix, no less, being part of the final day.

In 1970, Jimi Hendrix was to be on the bill alongside The Moody Blues at another momentous festival: the Isle of Wight. At this gathering on an island just off the south coast of England, there were even more people, somewhere in the region of 600,000. It was said to be one of the largest human gatherings in the world. Miles Davies, The Who, The Doors and Joni Mitchell were among those legendary artists performing with the band I now play with. As I type this, I can't help but feel I was born 20 years too late.

Although by comparison the behaviour tonight at The Moody Blues concert was slightly less anarchic, it did not deter the thousands here from enjoying the show. Seeing the looks of rapture on people's faces from the stage, as they hear the music of their youth, performed by the people who composed it, is nothing short of a privilege. And for this backing musician to play at this legendary venue, with this legendary band, under these circumstances, goes a long way to creating the feeling of exultation described above.

The band's sound system, equipment and instruments (drums and all) easily filled the 7,500-square-foot stage, and the view from the drum stool into the amphitheatre was dramatic indeed. From my advantageous seat I could clearly see the 4,500 seat pavilion, which was full, and beyond that, a sloping lawn accommodating a further 3,000 people. It would have been more, but due to some torrential rain earlier, we played to a total of 7,500 people – and what a sturdy bunch of fans they were on the lawn under umbrellas. Up on the horizon, once the rain stopped, the convivial concessions marquees created a beautiful silhouette against the setting sun as we played.

I have always been subject to a romantic longing to play at concerts like Bethel Woods, and on this occasion I was conclusively satisfied by the exciting evening. I caught a strong whiff of marijuana on a number of occasions from the audience, and while it wasn't a contributing factor, I doubt I would have enjoyed myself any more at the original festival.

## Postcard 29

FOR CORRESPONDENCE      FOR ADDRESS ONLY

Sunday
July 11th
2010

Stanley Theatre, Utica,
New York,
USA

I ended tonight's concert in a great deal of pain, caused by a minor accident that came about from the most unusual set of circumstances. In order to offer an explanation as to how this curious wound was inflicted I have to describe to the uninitiated exactly what a hi-hat is, so you can best understand how dangerous this little bugger can be if you find yourself on the wrong side of it.

The name hi-hat refers to the instrument operated by my left foot, which has two cymbals on top of it. You may recall in marching bands a musician holding two cymbals (one in each hand), and intermittently smashing them together for dramatic effect? Well, if you take those two cymbals, and stick them on top of a vertical stand, shove a metal pole down the middle attaching it to a foot plate, and then attach a spring to the top cymbal so that it moves up and down when you press the pedal, you have a hi-hat.

When your left foot presses down on the pedal, it pulls the top cymbal down onto the lower cymbal and chokes them together. When hit with a drumstick it makes a sort of 'chink' sound. If you continue to hit it as you slowly release your foot (like you would on, say, the clutch of a car) the cymbals gradually move apart, resulting in a much more 'swooshing' and loose sound when hit. If you take your foot completely off the pedal, the top cymbal stands proud of the lower cymbal by about four inches or so.

Now to the mishap. First imagine the hi-hat standing there with no one playing it: the two cymbals sit there silently, four inches apart, waiting for the drummer's left foot to stand on the pedal to bring our two items crashing together. Secondly, imagine a drummer (in this instance, me) standing up at the drum kit in order to play the other cymbals. In the second half of the show there is a song called *Isn't Life Strange*. My part consists of a series of cymbal swells, which I find are best performed when standing upright with the drum stool moved out of the way.

During tonight's performance at the Stanley Theatre in Utica, New York, I found myself fully engrossed in playing various cymbal swells as I made my way around the kit while standing up. At one point my back was to the hi-hat as I played a cymbal crescendo. On this occasion it had the inadvertent effect of momentarily throwing me off balance. I'm normally able to adjust my footing and maintain an upright position.

However, on this particular occasion I fell backwards very slightly, necessitating moving my right foot behind me to stop me from going any further. I couldn't see my right heel stepping onto the hi-hat pedal behind me, while simultaneously pushing my backside against the two open hi-hat cymbals. The combination of full body weight stamping on this unfortunately-placed pedal and an ample proportion of buttock flesh being forced in-between the gap of the two open hi-hat cymbals created a vice-like effect on my posterior, inflicting a pain that should never be experienced in that area; miraculously it didn't draw blood. The resulting wound (I found out later in the shower) resembled something of Dickensian proportions. It looked like a 19th century sadistic schoolmaster inflicted it with a horsewhip.

Returning to the topic of the Stanley Theatre in Utica, New York, the venue of this unfortunate occurrence: Utica is smack bang in the middle of New York state, and this utterly beautiful theatre is again one of those wonderfully ornate and historic buildings with an interior from an age of workmanship a far cry from what we see today. I found out from chatting to the stage doorman that the incredibly prolific theatre architect Thomas Lamb was responsible for the beautiful and lavish gold leaf interior, which he called 'Mexican Baroque' due to its unique blend in styles. This amazing establishment was first opened in September 1928 showing silent movies, and was also used to house a three manual Wurlitzer organ for silent movie accompaniment. I have a secret passion for theatre organs for some inexplicable reason. The organ was removed some time ago, but thankfully enthusiasts at Utica's Proctor High School still maintain it. Now that is something I would love to see, and had I had more time, I would have been finding my way there to play *Oh, I Do Like To Be Beside the Seaside* on it.

The theatre was quickly purchased just three days before its original opening by Warner Brothers, to become part of a chain of theatres under the same name, in order to get as many of their movies shown to as many people as possible simultaneously. Our venue for tonight had 2,945 seats, and as I painfully approached the end of our show with one cheek raised from the drum stool, I found myself thinking of all the performers from Gene Autry to Diana Ross, Aretha Franklin to Itzhak Perlman, who have sat (albeit a little more comfortably) on the same stage.

*Sunday*
*July 11th*
*2010*

*Danbury, Connecticut,*
*USA*

I have come down to The Good Ship Everything early today in order to sit here alone and write a little about our day off yesterday. However, my mind is rather preoccupied with the torrential rain, which is falling with such speed and volume as to create small and fast flowing rivers in the hotel car park where the bus is situated. Tonight we are playing, or rather should I say, are supposed to be playing, at an outdoor venue called the Ives Concert Park at Connecticut University. As it's completely uncovered, I am wondering exactly how many people will turn up. I have on occasions played to an audience of two nuns and a ferret, but never with this band. Over the years, however, The Moody Blues have played in all sorts of weather, with both the audience and the group steadfastly managing to muscle through, walking away with at least a pleasant if not altogether dry memory.

As concern for tonight's concert is at the forefront of my mind, I'm finding it difficult to concentrate on the finer details of the day off, including sitting beside the outdoor pool eating chicken salad... as interesting as it was. Equally, the morning, beginning with me lazily wandering over to Starbucks and ordering a green tea with a blueberry scone, then sitting comfortably in one of those big chairs in Barnes and Noble and reading for a couple of hours, is proving difficult to articulate in any meaningful way, although I know you are desperate to hear about it.

The four-hour journey to arrive at this hotel after the Utica show commenced with various small groups of performers converging at short intervals along the bus. Some were at the front with a glass of wine, others (including John and me) were standing in the middle section chatting, and a couple more were snoozing in the back. When the blinds on the bus are drawn and the lights are low it's a little bit like being in a submarine – encased in a long cylinder, communication with the outside world conducted via satellite. Even the door to the driver is closed at night, which completes the experience of total concealment inside our travelling metal tube.

On occasions the concept of being driven along like this falls into the subconscious, a little like flying. The only time you become consciously aware of this travelling phenomenon is when we hit what I would call land turbulence, and the bus rolls around, sending any passing occupants into a platonic embrace, for purposes of stability. It certainly makes for a close-knit group. Instead of sleeping on this journey, I did some 'hanging out' and managed to consume several glasses of rather delicious white wine, just enough to give me a cotton wool feeling inside my head.

Eventually we arrived, and I was once more into a hotel room at something o' clock in the morning. With suitcases tucked into the corner of the room and the lights turned off, I was ready to go to sleep, if only to rid myself of the self-inflicted heavy-headedness. According to the Book of Lies, this hotel was supposed to be a Marriott spa on the beach for us to have some R&R on a day off. It turned out to be nothing of the sort. I had a six-lane highway for a view, and an unusual window with no covering, meaning it let in an oblong shaft of light, not unlike the spotlight that illuminates me on stage. It is with a disappointment of almost biblical proportions that I discovered this beam of light was directed towards the bed, highlighting my sleeping position. The only thing missing was a film director shouting 'Action!'

You see, after a certain amount of time on the road, with constant travel, inconsistent food, a multitude of beds of differing quality, and living out of a suitcase for weeks, one's resolve can be tested. The philosophical approach to life, essential to a successful period in constant motion, can sometimes desert you at these moments.

Three o'clock in the morning, tired, ever so slightly drunk, and faced with a night of the wrong kind of enlightenment is enough to push even the most sophisticated road warrior over the edge. Moreover, with the exception of phoning down and complaining to some poor chap on night duty, there is not a lot you can do about it. I did manage to find an eye-mask from a plane at the bottom of my bag, and under the circumstances it worked a treat.

Fortunately the day off yesterday did offer sunshine, and with rest being my aim it was quite a success. Graeme and I went for a lovely dinner of lobster and steak (very romantic I must say) and of course by the second (or so) bottle of red wine, we managed to solve all of the world's political and economic problems in one sitting. If only the world leaders would be bothered to ask us at these elucidatory moments, humanity in its entirety would be saved.

Miraculously, after persuading the hotel to tape a big piece of cardboard over the offending window, creating a blackout effect, I managed to sleep for ten hours. Which brings me up to yet another hotel checkout, and to this early tour bus visit before anyone else arrives. When I am alone, The Good Ship Everything really is a wonderful place to write. Let's hope tonight's concert is not washed out; otherwise I fear I will be writing when I should be playing drums.

As I sit here, Norda and Alan have just boarded the bus following a trip over the road to get something to eat. This is where The Good Ship Everything really comes into its own. They look like a couple of *Titanic* extras and are currently attempting to change out of drenched clothes. It doesn't seem plausible that we'll be playing a concert in a few hours, because we currently resemble a washed out camping trip.

**Postcard 31**

FOR CORRESPONDENCE

FOR ADDRESS ONLY

Tuesday
July 13th
2010

Stamford, Connecticut,
USA
to
Ives Concert Park, Danbury,
Connecticut, USA
to
Philadelphia, Pennsylvania,
USA

Serie nº 711.4.5

As Coleridge said, it's a case of 'Water, water everywhere and not a drop to drink.' This really is a rock 'n' roll tour with a somewhat overly aquatic theme. The show tonight was literally in the middle of a small lake. Actually not what an American would call a lake, more like a pond. But the stretch of water was several hundred feet in diameter, which to a chap from England qualifies as a lake. The stage was most unusual: it resembled a cross between a giant cabana and a small pagoda floating in the water, not in the middle, but away from the water's edge to a degree that created at least a significant 'moat' in front of the stage, with the majority of remaining water behind.

The Ives Concert Park is billed as a 'prestigious, world-class performing arts centre' and given the position of this majestic outdoor amphitheatre set in 40 acres of woodland, it's difficult to argue with the description. However, you may recall the small matter of precipitation. Segueing from yesterday's observations, we found ourselves travelling the 55 miles of wet road cautiously, while observing the lead-grey skies. After what seemed to be a very long time, and with the blinds now drawn, The Good Ship Everything began to make the sort of slowing down noises that suggested imminent arrival. The weather at our destination was indubitably the same as when we set off, and the forecast wasn't suggesting any improvement.

I disembarked and walked to our cordoned-off outdoors quarters. The crew had done a magnificent job of setting up a series of trailers; mine was a very comfortable air-conditioned habitat to change in indeed. In fact it was bigger and better kitted-out than some apartments I've lived in. The catering company had set up just outside the door, and fresh cooked salmon along with a delicious vegetarian chilli were on the menu from an extremely jolly and resourceful chef called Jenny. She was going about her business as if catering for a crew of 30 and a group of rock musicians, under a canopy in the pouring rain, in the middle of 40 acres of woodland, was an everyday occurrence. It was all rather bohemian.

I walked in the direction of the stage, 'savouring' the odour of the portable toilets en route, and found the huge wooden structure out in the water where we were to perform. Tarpaulin and plastic sheeting were everywhere. Of course I had completely underestimated the crew, who had erected several hundred tonnes of sound equipment, lights, instruments; laid carpet, set up various stations next to the stage for tuning, etc. – the usual stuff, but all in the rain. The weather had hardly made a difference. I'm telling you these guys are made of different stuff to you and me – well maybe not you, but certainly me.

With all the performance paraphernalia taken care of, we were still left with the little matter of the audience due to be sitting under the stars (I mean heavy clouds). From our cordoned-off area, which was a veritable circle of wagons tied together with assorted coverings, I could see the audience filing into the grounds – many more than I would have thought possible, with each in possession of the considered apparel of serious concertgoers (folding chairs, umbrellas, coolers etc.) - very impressive. Maybe the concert was not only going to go ahead, but it was beginning to look like it might have the makings of a success.

Remarkably the rain ceased for us to start the concert on time, and once again as if nothing were out of the ordinary, we began on time at 8.10pm and launched once more into the now very well rehearsed set. For some reason the sound on stage (by which I mean in my in-ear monitors) was crystal clear, which makes a huge difference to the enjoyment of a show for me. And the thousands of people in the audience were enjoying the show as if it were a sunny evening, or at least they appeared to be from my drum stool. After the fourth song, I saw ascending umbrellas among the crowd, followed by yellow concert cagoules being pulled over wet bodies. Although it wasn't falling directly onto the stage (which was the only covered area) it had started to rain yet again. It became clear this wasn't just a shower but a full-on deluge, completely saturating anyone not on stage.

I could see gallons of water passing through the tubes of spotlights pointing at the stage: not the sort of rain you see falling, more like a giant waterfall with the audience underneath it. Within seconds local crew were running past me, oblivious to the music, pulling plastic sheeting over the speakers and anything electrical. An assortment of activity ensued while we continued to play, seemingly to the delight of the crowd, some of whom looked like they had swam to get to their seats.

Thankfully, after a short while the rain stopped and we carried on to the end of the show to the rapturous applause of the crowd.

We ended on our usual high despite the weather, leaving only three more shows to do on this leg of the tour.

Today was one of those tri-city days, starting in Stamford, Connecticut, moving on to the waterlogged Ives Concert Park in Danbury in the same state, and arriving very late in Philadelphia to an absolutely wonderful hotel where the beds were heavenly. It was a long day indeed, but after a warm shower and a perfect bed to climb into, 3.30am didn't feel too bad at all.

Philadelphia is one of the first major cities I visited in the US, and it was a long time ago – 1979. I was 19 and it was my inaugural trip abroad. Without going into detail at this point, The City of Brotherly Love was my first real taste of a big city anywhere. And here I am 31 years later, having visited the city nearly every year for the past 20 years. I feel every bit at home as if I were in London, with maybe just a little bit of additional rock 'n' roll excitement.

**Postcard 32**

FOR CORRESPONDENCE

FOR ADDRESS ONLY

Wednesday
July 14th
2010

Philadelphia, Pennsylvania,
USA
to
The Mayo Center for the Performing
Arts, Morristown,
New Jersey, USA
(and back again)

I love waking up in a new city after arriving in the early hours of the morning, and as Philadelphia is one of those cities I know rather well, it has the added advantage of an air of familiarity. Depending on which hotel I am staying at, I know exactly which direction to walk to get to the nearest café, museum or place of interest. When I first started touring with The Moody Blues, I made it my business to sniff out as many local jazz clubs as I possibly could. In the early days of my tenure with the group I was walking around the city one morning and spotted a jazz club advertising a performance that night by the Tony Williams Quartet. Now, for the uninitiated, Tony Williams was widely regarded as one of the most important and influential jazz drummers to come to prominence in the 1960s, playing with the trumpeter Miles Davis.

I cannot tell you how excited I was at the opportunity to see one of my heroes play live in America. It also happened to be a day off for us in Philadelphia, so I rushed back to the hotel in excited fashion to tell the rest of the band about my find. At that time in the early 1990s, The Moody Blues employed five backing musicians, including myself, Bias Boshell, Paul Bliss, Sue Shattock and June Boyce. While none of them were the slightest bit interested in old jazz drummers, I was clearly enthusiastic enough for us all, and although John, Justin, Graeme and Ray declined my offer, I managed to round up the somewhat reluctant remaining musicians to go to the club that evening.

The fact that Tony Williams was one of the world's most revered jazz giants, and this was a small club in Philadelphia, did seem a little odd. However, as jazz is not renowned for selling huge amounts of tickets, I thought nothing more of it — especially as I had recently seen on *The Simpsons,* a poster that said, 'Jazz music — 14 people can't be wrong.'

I distinctly remember collecting $15 from each of my companions and handing it over to the doorman, whom I could have sworn was George Foreman, then rushing ahead to secure some seats close to the front. I was like a child on a trip to Disneyland; settling into my seat, in my delight I ordered five Piña coladas, all the while enthusing to my colleagues and bleating, 'Don't worry, this is going to be great.' In my eagerness we had arrived early, and we were on our third round of drinks (maybe fourth) before the band came on. The announcement for the Tony Williams Quartet was met with a polite smattering of applause from the majority of the audience, apart from one of only five white people sitting at the front clapping in an almost maniacal fashion.

Four musicians walked onstage, and I don't want to say they were awfully young but one of them was wearing a school uniform... and he sat at the drum kit. Then the awful truth hit me like a cold wet fish in the face. This wasn't the Tony Williams of Miles Davis, Herbie Hancock and John McLaughlin fame, who was responsible for the beginnings of jazz-fusion, and who helped redefine the role of the jazz rhythm section through the use of polyrhythms and metric modulation, the drummer I had spent years listening to; this was a local saxophone player who I later found out was a police cadet. This Tony Williams Quartet were not only not very good, they were awful. It didn't take long for one of the backing singers to lean over and say 'Marshall, what is this shit?' Needless to say they left immediately with looks of disdain, mumbling insults not at all under their breath, along with phrases like 'I'll get my money back from you tomorrow', and the like.

I decided to stay on my own, in a feeble attempt to pretend there was something worthwhile in what they were trying to do, but to say the music was bad is to pay them a compliment. I managed to stay until the first interval, but when I found out the children on stage had not even heard of the real Tony Williams, I bid my farewell and left in a melancholy frame of mind.

Moving forward to the current day, jazz clubs have become a thing of legend (and of the past) amongst the band. When we arrive at hotels after a show, at 2.00am or 3.00am or thereabouts, I often volunteer 'Jazz club anyone?' which is normally met with 'Yeah, great Gordy... you go and get the drinks in, I'll just pop to my room and get eight hours sleep and I'll see you there.'

We set off today to drive to the Community Theatre (also known as the Mayo Center for the Performing Arts) in Morristown, New Jersey. It's a really small but intensely beautiful theatre with a capacity of just 1,300, and although it's set out like a theatre it has the intimate atmosphere of a club. This is the final push to the end of our US trip, and if it's possible, the concerts are gaining momentum with fans trying to make the final few shows.

I knew the theatre was built originally in 1937 by Walter Read as a motion picture house, so I was taken completely by surprise by the backstage technical facilities, including an amazing fly-rail system, some brand-new dressing rooms all air-conditioned, and a general brand-spanking-new feel to the place. It turns out that in March of this year the theatre completed a $7 million upgrade, and for once you can see where the money has gone. While maintaining its plush look, it has the air of brand-new premises. The fact that it's a community theatre guarantees wide usage from major artists to local schools.

I'm now back at our hotel in Philadelphia, and just about to take a wander out into the streets to soak up the atmosphere in what is one of my final days this year in America.

My jogging adventures have stopped over the past week due to the heatwave here in North America this summer. Even sauntering around Philadelphia today proved to be heavy work, although it was well worth it. I took a stroll along Arch Street, then down 5th Street to the Philadelphia City Hall, one of my favourite all-time American City Halls. It was designed by the Scottish-born architect John McArthur at around the turn of the 20th century, and was built to be the world's tallest building. Although the Eiffel Tower surpassed it by the time it was completed (trust the French), it did remain the largest 'habitable building' in the world for some time.

I first visited this huge limestone and marble building with its granite and marble walls (which had to be 22 feet thick since they weren't made of steel) in 1979, and it is still as staggeringly beautiful to me today as it was 31 years ago. The entrance alone, which consists of huge pillars on top of huge pillars, on top of huge pillars, is not only an astonishing triumph of construction but also a magnificent sight. Now, of course, it sits amongst other more modern buildings scraping the sky. This means that any visitor (even one as frequent as me) walks around with their head pointing to the sky, as if they're trying to balance a garden chair on their forehead.

It's one of the most dramatic skylines, and if it could speak it would shout 'America' – I love it.

My plan was to be at the Reading Terminal Market for breakfast, but as we were in so late from the last night's gig, it was not until midday that I found myself heading off, so technically the upcoming feast was more lunch than breakfast. The market is a unique food hall and is housed in a huge enclosed space with a low roof. It used to be the train shed of the Reading Train Terminal. Now it's a bustling, restless group of nearly a hundred merchants offering an eclectic array of groceries, baked goodies, crafts and ethnic foods – there was even an Amish gentleman laying out fresh corn for sale.

Walking through the doors of the market I saw a swirl of humanity, with all sorts of colourful characters in attendance, and, I would imagine, it's a perfect working environment for a pickpocket. In two separate designated eating areas, there were musicians playing for tips that listeners could deposit in the jars provided. At one end a very casually dressed African-American man in sunglasses and flip-flops was playing stride piano (a rendition of *Tea for Two* as I passed the first time), and at the other end, a duo consisting of a singer/ guitarist and violinist was playing country music. These musical offerings lent it an altogether unique atmosphere of originality and imaginativeness, in addition to the normal ambient noise associated with such a place.

Finding it very difficult to make up my mind whether to go for the salt beef stand or sushi – or anything, for that matter – I happened upon a very fresh-looking Mexican food stall, so my breakfast became chicken mole burrito and guacamole. As I sat there finishing the first meal of the day, I placed my elbows on the table and clasped my hands together - just try this now for me if you

will? Put your elbows on a table, and clasp your fingers together...
stick your thumbs out and rest your chin on the thumbs.

It's a position I adopt when in silent contemplation. However, my
fingers wouldn't slide in between each other, which was curious.

Upon closer inspection I realised they were extremely swollen.
It's a regular happening on tour, but I'm not always conscious of it
until I try this particular meditative pose.

It manifests when I have been playing hard – gripping a pair of
sticks and bashing drums and cymbals thousands of times a night
means my hands look rather like a pair of World Cup goalie's
gloves. It's a conspicuous phenomenon that soon wears off, but as I
sat inside this old train-shed-cum-market in downtown Philadelphia,
eating Mexican food for breakfast and listening to stride piano by a
man in flip-flops and sunglasses, not being able to clasp my hands
together struck me (and I don't know why) as a singularly bizarre
moment in life.

I wandered back through the familiar streets of Philadelphia in
the heavy humidity; it was the sort of heat that extracts all energy
within minutes. An old bookshop took my attention, so I entered,
but as it wasn't air-conditioned I didn't last long in there. Refuge was
taken in a women's clothing shop on the way back to the hotel, so I
decided to do some shopping. Not for me, I hasten to add, but for
my re-entry tax.

The 're-entry tax' is a collection of gifts you take home to
appease family members for having been absent for so long. I
can't claim credit for the expression, as it's one of those colloquial
phrases used by touring musicians that appears to have been around
forever. Of course I love to take presents home at the end of every
tour. Anyway – although this shop was air-conditioned and had

the added advantage of being populated with young and attractive sales assistants, I was still lacking the energy to make any type of purchasing decision. I ambled back to the hotel and readied myself for the show instead.

This, our penultimate concert, was at the familiar State Theatre Center for the Arts, in Easton, Pennsylvania, which is equidistant between Philadelphia and New York City, both about 70 miles away. Similar to the previous night, this small and atmospheric setting is very much a community theatre with an assortment of performers passing through from rock 'n' roll tours, to musical theatre and plays.

The atmosphere tonight was absolutely electric, and we walked on to a standing ovation. It's the sort of statement that suggests the audience are already enjoying themselves, and puts the band at a huge advantage; insofar as long as you do your job, you're pretty much onto a winner. Tonight's show was one of the first to go on sale for this tour, and it sold out immediately. Pennsylvania has always been a popular area for the band to play, which this concert confirmed.

**Postcard 34**

FOR CORRESPONDENCE          FOR ADDRESS ONLY

*Friday*
*July 16th*
*2010*

*Borgata Center.*
*Atlantic City.*
*New Jersey. USA*

Serie N° 714 4.8

It finally arrived: our closing concert this year on American soil (in addition to our four shows on Canadian soil of course). After driving 6,886 miles (give or take) in 30 days, covering two countries, travelling through 14 states, visiting 25 cities and playing 24 concerts, our final destination was the Borgata Hotel in Atlantic City. While this extraordinary New Jersey city is famous for its boardwalk and casinos, it also has some quite marvellous beaches, and from the top floor of this entertainment centre, the view of the Atlantic Ocean is quite something.

The Borgata in Atlantic City has become a regular venue in which The Moody Blues perform. The list of artists who regularly appear here reads like yet another *Who's Who* of the music industry. Along with The Moody Blues, posters of Elton John, David Bowie, Rod Stewart, John Mellencamp, Stevie Wonder, The Who, Eric Clapton, Lenny Kravitz, Billy Joel, the Eagles, Santana and Sting are just some of the artists lining the walls outside our dressing room.

The backstage area is part of an interconnected labyrinth of corridors that requires a veritable A to Z map to navigate. Thankfully our crew used orange duct tape to create arrows on the floor and walls to direct everybody to the stage, dressing rooms, catering and the exit. Along each of these routes are endless framed posters of even more artists who have performed here since its opening. Our audience consists of regional fans that attend a few concerts, alongside some who, incredibly, never miss a performance. Together they make up a sold-out audience.

We set off for the 90-mile trip to Atlantic City in the early afternoon heat. I moved quickly from the hotel to the air conditioned Good Ship Everything trying not to perspire in a fresh shirt. I was carrying an extra bag today, as I wanted to collect a few things from the flight-cased wardrobe, which follows me around and miraculously turns up in every dressing room and trailer at each show. Items returning home with me include an extra flute, in case I sit on the main flute and bend it in half or otherwise render it somehow unplayable, and a small portable practice pad attached to a mini tripod that I use to warm up before a show.

The practice pad has been with me for more years than I care to remember; it's essentially a flat six-inch diameter piece of silicone which is, I believe, the same material that was used to enlarge the breasts of a lady I once saw, hanging upside down on a pole by her legs only, wearing a piece of pink dental floss where her underwear would normally be, from whence a certain well known low-denomination currency was protruding, in an establishment of extremely overpriced drinks, er... sorry, where was I? Oh yes, my practice pad. I spend at least 30 minutes before a show pretending this pad is a drum, and as the silicone surface doesn't make much of a sound when I hit it, I can thwack away playing drum rudiments to my heart's content without having other band members telling me to be quiet while simultaneously hurling loose objects in my direction. This warm-up pad goes with me everywhere, so I brought it back to the hotel for it to accompany me to the UK.

After the final show of a tour, there is always a slight sense of anticlimax. We have all shared a multitude of emotions; some are vivid, some wistful, some poignant, some profound. It feels like there should be a debriefing in order to exit this institution that is a rock 'n' roll tour. However, we are all looking forward to going home – we all have things to do, and the next leg of the tour begins in the UK in only six weeks; it feels confusingly more like bon voyage than goodbye.

We will save the big farewells until the end of the tour proper in September. In the meantime, we all board The Good Ship Everything for the final journey back to the hotel, as tomorrow we go our separate ways until we meet again in London. The 90-mile return journey did feel like a debriefing, with everyone recounting particular anecdotes from the many situations we've found ourselves in over the past 30 days; a warm feeling of accomplishment travelled along with our small group of musicians.

Together with Udo, Julie and John, back at the hotel I enjoyed a single whisky in the bar, just to wind down conclusively, you understand. I slept like never before – a full nine hours from when my head hit the pillow to me waking in exactly the same position at 10.00am. My flight was not until later in the day, so having a few hours completely to myself, I used it to the full, with a visit to the Benjamin Franklin Memorial Centre. They had a travelling exhibit entitled 'Cleopatra, the Search for the Last Queen of Egypt,' and I spent most of my time looking at the Heracleion, which are two 16-foot-tall colossal figures of a Ptolemaic king and queen from the Temple of Amon at Heracleion.

I used to spend my final day of a rock tour trying to open my eyelids, with a pounding head due to the superabundant and celebratory consumption of tequila some hours before. How things have changed. Now I gain far more pleasure from seeking out exhibits of ancient civilizations and reading books. Ah well, rock 'n' roll.

After a quick workout in the gym, I packed my cases one last time while waiting for an extortionately priced turkey burger from room service. Lobby call was at 3.30pm, and a car then took me to the Philadelphia airport to catch the red-eye back to Heathrow, where I arrived the following day at 6.20am. I'm now sitting at the dining table in my conservatory back in Wimbledon, with a green tea and an 'everything' bagel, finishing this postcard.

**Postcard 35**

FOR CORRESPONDENCE     FOR ADDRESS ONLY

Sunday
July 18th
2010

London,
UK

Of course this is not the end of the story — we have just come to a gap in the proceedings. Our investigation into the world of a rock 'n' roll tour continues when we begin production rehearsals in Brighton, UK, on September 6th, which is a little over six weeks away. So before I move on, let me say — without wanting to sound too sycophantic — how much I love the USA and can't wait to go back.

There are many differences between touring the US and touring the UK. Both ventures have upsides and downsides, mostly to do with how people communicate. I very much admire the positive 'can do' attitude of Americans, whereas the English display a much more subtle — some would say 'concealed' — welcome.

However... there is just one form of American exchange that I simply do not understand, and that is the rhetorical greeting. Take for instance the very first banter of the day between our bus driver, David, and Alan (both Americans). It would begin with Alan saying 'Heywhatchyagotgoin?' which I believe translates to 'Hello, what have you got going?' to which David does not directly answer but instead replies with another question: 'Heywassup?' – 'Hello, what is up?' Now although I can successfully translate, I am unable to offer any clear explanation as to the meaning of this greeting. If I am caught in the middle of one of these curious interactions, I find the only option is to throw a further anomaly into the mix, something along the lines of 'Howsithangin?' hoping beyond hope that my contribution will not be answered.

It's all conducted with a big friendly smile, and often with some body part (usually the shoulder) being slapped or pushed in a friendly but significant manner. I like it, but I just don't understand it.

This tour has been typical of the countless expeditions undertaken with The Moody Blues over the past 20 years, and although it is an unusual method of earning a living, it certainly doesn't feel like work for the two and a half hours we spend on stage. There has always been another tour scheduled into the future, as this is what we do.

Of course at some point it will stop, but just not yet. The UK leg of the tour is just around the corner, so until that time I bid you a brief farewell.

**Postcard 36**

Tuesday
September 7th
2010

Brighton Centre.
Brighton.
UK

So, here we are – the next section of the tour: a trip that originally began in the US and is now resuming on this sunny autumn morning in the UK. This portion is going to be rather gruelling because of the amount of road travel. Glancing through the Book Of Lies, it appears we will be 'hitting and running' lots of the concerts, and returning to London after most of the shows. It means I get to come home, of course, which is a major plus to this itinerant minstrel; but it also requires many hours of travel on the unsympathetic British roads.

Our bus for this part of the tour is the UK equivalent of The Good Ship Everything. However, as we are not doing any proper overnight journeys on this bus, it becomes The Good Ship Almost Everything. It's smaller by design – as most vehicles tend to be in Europe – but it still has a big horseshoe leather seat in the back lounge, with a flat screen TV, a hard drive full of more movies than we could possibly watch in a year, never mind one UK tour, and all the facilities one would expect on a vehicle catering to a rock band... you know the sort of thing: cheese sandwiches, bottles of wine, hot and cold running women, etc.

Graeme and I commandeered the rear of the vehicle, commonly known as the 'bad boys' lounge,' due to the fact that two drummers occupy it. However, if the truth be known, the worst that generally happens back there are some exaggerated touring anecdotes, and the consumption of an excess of chocolate biscuits with maybe a 'shoot 'em up' movie thrown in.

## The morning of the first day

This day of work began with production rehearsals at our first venue: The Brighton Centre. For many reasons Brighton is one of my favourite seaside resorts, partly because I have some amazing memories of the place, but also because it is such a picturesque town. It is the setting of some fascinating landmarks: the Royal Pavilion (the former royal residence) for one, with its Islamic architecture as an exterior, Far Eastern internal décor, and an enchanting skyline, along with a couple of piers, one of which was burned down in a dramatic blaze in 2003.

Brighton has everything one requires for a short vacation in the summer: lovely beaches, a plethora of commendable restaurants, and a very agreeable shopping area known as The Lanes, which has funky, bespoke clothes and antique shops along narrow lanes. And this enthusiastic description comes from someone who becomes deeply dispirited at the thought of spending more than a few minutes in a shop. It also has a nudist beach.

We all pitched up at the theatre to begin a day of rehearsal. It's only now that we find out we have a different monitor guy for this leg of the tour – a young chap named Simon, who is clearly capable and experienced, but has not worked with us before. The job of monitor guy, incidentally, is one of the most stressful of occupations in the music business. Whoever takes this job has to be both very, very good at what they do, and also (just as importantly) extremely thick-skinned.

For those of you unacquainted with this critical role, let me tell you, you wouldn't want to be one unless you had gonads of steel, the disposition of a Zen master, the ability to be able to take continual criticism from exasperated and irritated musicians who don't think you are any good at your job (even when you are), and be in full possession of the workings of the sound desk in front of you, which has more knobs and buttons on it than a NASA space shuttle. You also need to have eyes in the back of your head, be able to lip read in the dark from the side of the stage through clouds of dry smoke, and be musical. Apart from that it's a doddle of a job. Oh, one other thing – when you turn up as a new kid, with an established band who are used to everything being perfect and do not suffer fools lightly, and things go wrong, all of these previous virtues count for nothing. You're done for.

This made our young Simon all the more impressive to me, as today he was dealt a very difficult situation – some would say impossible. Bear with me for a minute while I briefly explain the responsibilities of Monitor Guy and the ramifications of him doing something wrong. When you play in a loud rock band, it can be very difficult to hear a vocalist from, say, the other side of the stage, especially if guitar amplifiers are in the way. We used to get round this challenge by each having our own speakers close by with a mix of the band coming though it, so we all stood a chance of playing in time, or at least playing the same song.

Nowadays, technology has moved on and we have in-ear monitoring, which is the same principle, but we use custom-moulded earpieces instead of a speaker to feed the desired mix directly into our ears. The principle is simply fantastic: when you're playing on stage and you want to hear the flute over the other side of the stage, you simply ask Monitor Guy to turn the flute microphone up in your 'in-ears,' and Bob's your auntie. It doesn't matter what's going on elsewhere; there could be a military coup being conducted by the audience and you would only hear beautiful waves of melodic woodwind music whispering delicately in your ear. Everything is wonderful with this system, until it goes wrong.

If the mix in the in-ear monitors is amiss or somehow out of balance, it can make it impossible to play in time as a group. It causes what's known in the business as 'horse's eyes.' This is the expression a musician adopts while playing, when he wishes to ask the question, 'Where the fuck are we?' What can follow is the musical equivalent of a train crash.

All of our mixes are digitally programmed and saved onto a USB stick, which Monitor Guy then inserts into the monitor desk, enabling us to have the same mixes wherever we are in the world.

Needless to say as we started running through the first song, everybody's individual pre-programmed in-ear monitor mix was completely different to what it should have been. Somehow the data on the USB stick had been corrupted and the mixes were all over the place. All eyes were on Simon. He hadn't done anything, of course, but it was his responsibility to put it right.

The poor chap now had a veritable crisis on his hands; add to that the fact that he is 14 years of age (he may be slightly older than that, but he looked 14 to me) and you get an idea of the challenge facing him. However, he methodically worked though everyone's mix, and without succumbing to the looks of mild panic from the band, managed to solve the entire problem during the rehearsal.

So the show went ahead tonight, just as though we had played in Philadelphia the night before. Except instead of going back to a hotel after the gig, we drove back to London, and I climbed into my own bed. Luxury.

**Postcard 37**

FOR CORRESPONDENCE · FOR ADDRESS ONLY

*Tuesday*
*September 7th*
*2010*

*Plymouth Pavilions,*
*Plymouth,*
*UK*

Do you want to know how long we were on the tour bus today? Well, I'll tell you: long enough to watch six episodes of *Band Of Brothers*, and stop for lunch on the way. After our prolonged journey, we arrived at the Plymouth Pavilions in Devon. As I was stepping down from the bus, memories instantly flooded my mind, including a long-forgotten family holiday, and a stint with a travelling production of *Joseph and the Amazing Technicolor Dreamcoat* during an earlier, less successful period of my career.

As a result of the latter of these two recollections, I had a distinct flashback of arriving here in 1981 for a two-week engagement in Joseph with my best friend and guitarist, Andy Holdsworth, and having to find our own 'digs,' or lodgings. The way it worked was that upon arriving at the theatre with the prospect of playing thirteen shows a week (two shows a day from Monday to Friday and three shows on Saturday), we would scour the notice board at the stage door for cards that read 'Theatrical Digs.' This term sparked a romantic notion for me which was quickly dispelled when I reached the house offering board and lodgings.

Theatrical digs can often be wonderful, home-from-home type hostelries, with plump comforts and welcoming landladies. Be that as it may, there is always an element of unpredictability when choosing theatrical digs, especially if it's the last one left on the notice board at stage door. This was the case when Andy and I played here for our fateful two-week engagement.

We arrived at the substantial-looking double-fronted house, which appeared decidedly promising. The landlady, a plump and rosy-cheeked woman of about 50 years of age, showed us through the house, past a most comfortable-looking lounge, and into a country-style kitchen at the back. I looked at Andy with one of those sideways facial expressions where the eyebrows raise up high, and the sides of the mouth point down as if to say 'this is looking good' – and at £25 per week we weren't going to complain.

Curiously and without breaking step, she continued through the back door and into the garden, where she showed us to an out-building with a corrugated roof. We were suddenly in what appeared to be camping territory. To Andy's horror there was only one small bed, something I didn't care about all that much, but which clearly sent Andy into state of unease. I must point out that this was in the winter, and the weather was unpredictable to say the least. In the afternoon sunshine the full horror of what was to await us was not apparent, and would not become so until later that night, when we came in from the show.

I can't remember the show exactly on that night, although we always had fun. As two best mates barely out of our teens and touring together, we were always engaged in endless tomfoolery and mirth. I think we probably spent more money on beer than we earned, but at that age we were immortal. It wasn't until we staggered back to the digs from celebrating the opening night in Plymouth after a hearty attempt at being thrown out of the pub (we succeeded I believe) that it dawned on us we were sleeping outside that night. We would be covered, but be in no doubt – we were essentially al fresco.

We silently negotiated our way through the boarding house, somehow managing to knock over the milk bottles by the front door and a potted plant in the hallway, continuing to trip over each other as we fell out the back door, and made our way into the garden. There was no lock on the door to our meagre dwellings, and the wind had blown it open, so we walked in and closed the door behind us. It looked completely different in the dark. One single bedside light and no heating – this really was a converted potting shed.

Both musicians got into bed fully clothed, as stripping off in these conditions was simply not an option. It was then it began to rain, and rain hard. You may remember I mentioned a corrugated roof? Well, this is where it came into its own. The rain pattered against the corrugated roof like a landslide of heavy pebbles. Laying on his back, shivering with the covers tucked tightly under his chin, watching the steam coming out of his mouth, Andy said, 'That's louder than your fucking drum kit.' Within minutes we were cold, full of woe and ineffably miserable. I lay there telling myself that one day, this would be 30 years ago.

And so it was 30 years later that I stepped from The Moody Blues' tour bus into the crisp sunshine of this autumnal day, where I was met by our tour manager who showed me the way to my dressing room, and then directed me to catering. What a difference a few decades can make.

I determined it would be a good idea to go for a little jog before tonight's show to warm up my limbs, due to stiffness from having been on the bus for so many hours. So I set off in my new New Balance running shoes (I had to cremate the Nikes from Chicago) and ran down towards the sea along West Hoe Road. The weather was a combination of Indian summer sun and fresh sea air, and was simply gorgeous. I cruised on foot with a light heart down to the Tinside Lido, breathing in the scenic views, and studied the outline of Drake's Island, a small but fetching 6.5 acres of volcanic tuff and lava lying in the waters of Plymouth Sound.

The Plymouth/Roscoff ferry sailed in the distance, and a group of young boys were playing with a ball in the sea, just outside the lido. It was a perfect setting, and my mood was greatly elevated in comparison to the memories of my earlier visit here all those years ago.

Now getting hungry, I made my way back to the venue, and after stretching, sat down in catering to a first class meal of fishcakes and chunky chips with tartar sauce, and polished it off with chocolate cake. I promptly fell fast asleep in the dressing room for 30 minutes, woke up about 45 minutes before the show and showered. I changed and stretched once more, and in my rested, well fed and post-workout high, I walked on stage with a feeling of quiet exaltation.

The concert in Plymouth was outstanding. It felt good, I felt good, it sounded great, and the audience appeared to love every minute of it. I've lost count of how many times I have mentioned how satisfying it is to play this show, but I find it difficult to talk about performing when I feel like this, without becoming just a little bit overenthusiastic.

After the show tonight, we celebrated Udo's birthday; we ate cake off paper plates and drank champagne out of plastic glasses on the bus on the way home. Well, when I say we had champagne, we spilled most of it on the floor, transferring the refreshment from bottle to glass as the bus rolled around, but we all had a sip.

Since flying over from the US to begin this tour, we have completed a long production rehearsal in Brighton; driven back to London; driven back down to Brighton to play a concert; and then driven six hours to Plymouth. It's now 2.00am. With all this activity it's hard to believe we have only performed two concerts. As I finish this postcard I think we are playing Cardiff tomorrow. It's not a good sign that I've lost my bearings already.

## Postscript

Andy Holdsworth and I are still best friends. He is now a photographer; the guitarist in the musical *Billy Elliot* in London's West End; and also plays guitar with me in Jeff Wayne's *The War of the Worlds*.

**Postcard 38**

FOR CORRESPONDENCE     FOR ADDRESS ONLY

*Thursday*
*September 9th*
*2010*

*London,*
*UK*

Normally when on tour, I am away from my home and I stay in a hotel. This is a 24-hours-a-day, seven-days-a-week job, with the most important part of the day being 8.00pm, or whenever the concert begins. When I'm based out of various hotels this is relatively easy – when I'm based at home it becomes rather a different story. I will for a moment attempt to elucidate.

On the road, as I have illustrated in previous postcards, life is rather like being in an institution. The daily decisions of what to eat, what to do, where to go, etc. are for the most part removed, and in its place is a detailed schedule that requires nothing more than total, almost religious adherence. What touring requires is for the incumbent hired musician to tailor his day around the evening's performance. Most people tend to be at work around 8.00am; we, on the other hand, have to be at work at 8.00pm, which influences the rest of the day's activities.

Firstly, it means a completely different bedtime, eating roster, and exercise program. Any recreation is fitted around this alternative timetable. Consider the difference to being at home: with an alarm set on weekdays at 6.30am for the children to get up for school and my wife to go to work, evening meals are eaten between 6.00pm and 8.00pm, and bedtime is normally 11.00pm.

As much as I love being at home with my family, it's a tricky thing to do mid-tour when work and family life are operating in different time zones. It's very difficult to return home after a several hundred-mile journey, climb into bed at 3.00am and then hear the morning alarm three and a half hours later. This morning I heard the house awaken. My daughters were readying themselves for school, and Harley, our dog, was scampering about. These are the wonderful homely sounds I miss when I'm on a tour bus in the US, but now I lay listening through semi-consciousness as my too-few hours of sleep were being disturbed. By the time the house was calm and there was an eerie silence, it was just about time to wake up and go to meet the tour bus.

Not to fear, as today is a day off and I can relax... or so I thought. As I will do almost anything to keep my daughters in tap shoes, I have a 'say yes to everything' philosophy when it comes to being offered work. So when I received a phone call from Accy, the percussionist in the West End show *Thriller Live* asking if I would I like to pop into town and play the show for him, I decided to take the job. This effectively ended my day off.

In order to get there, today's Good Ship Everything was Greater London Transport's number 163 bus from the bottom of my road, which got me to Wimbledon Station in about ten minutes. I took the train to Waterloo, and from there, it was three stops on the underground to Piccadilly Circus, and a short walk to the stage door of the Lyric Theatre to play in Michael Jackson's *Thriller Live*.

It's quite different to playing with The Moody Blues, although it is most enjoyable. The band is an ever-changing group of top session musicians, and tonight I played percussion and keyboards. When the show finished I literally ran back to Piccadilly Circus for the return journey, and arrived back home at 11.00pm.

The following day was when the true challenge of being on tour/at home emerged. Although my family fully understood my nocturnal timetable and left me in bed, it didn't feel right, so I got up. My in-laws, who are truly delightful, were visiting London, and they came round for brunch. This means I spent an extremely pleasant few hours surrounded by familial warmth, eating smoked salmon and scrambled egg with bagels washed down with some delicious coffee.

Playing in *Thriller Live* in the days leading up to this tour meant I'd played ten days in a row now without a break. Tomorrow The Moody Blues play in Cardiff, and we are staying in a hotel for the night. Perhaps then I might be able to discard this sleep deprivation, and catch up on some much needed shut-eye. I think this is called 'living the dream.'

**Postcard 39**

Friday
September 10th
2010

London
to
St. David's Hall.
Cardiff. Wales

The alarm went off as expected at 6.30am at my home in London, and today we played Cardiff. My wife left me in bed in order for me to have a few additional hours' sleep, but my youngest daughter came up and gently asked me to come downstairs and cover some of her schoolbooks with sticky-back plastic. With only one eye open and morning hair, I gingerly made my way downstairs, squinting like Mr Magoo. I was met with a bright and breezy bunch of members of my immediate family, employed in the serious business of getting ready for school and work. Although I was observing these domestic activities through a sleepy haze, I eventually emerged into semi-consciousness.

A whirlwind of 30 minutes passed and within what seemed like seconds the house was empty. Harley (the dog) and I were left sitting in silence surrounded by the debris of a hurried school morning breakfast. It was quite an out-of-body experience, and in this moment I did not at all feel like a rock star. Harley had spent the entire summer in the Lake District, and was still trying (not always successfully) to get used to London. She followed me around the house like a shadow, inspecting everything I did.

I had to be awake early this morning anyway, for a 9.00am

meeting at the bank to open a business account for my newly formed company. I made myself a strong cup of tea and managed to consume nearly the entire contents of a bowl of cereal before attempting some cursory ablutions. I dressed myself in conservative clothes in an attempt to look less like a drummer on tour and more like someone who would be presentable to a bank.

When I turned up to the meeting, a very pleasant gentleman with a fastidious manner took me through the lengthy process of opening a bank account. It appeared to me that 80 per cent of the meeting was quite irrelevant, and the piece of paper I signed at the end took seconds. However, with the job done I returned home. A taxi arrived on time to get me to the meeting point for The Good Ship Almost Everything for our trip to Cardiff. I would be spending the next three nights away from home, so it dawned on me I should really pack something, such as clean underwear, a toothbrush, a good book and maybe an emergency banana.

After completing a man's version of cleaning the kitchen, and throwing various non-specific items of clothing into a small case, I climbed into the taxi. Within 30 minutes I was happily ensconced on the tour bus en route to Cardiff.

Our catering company for this trip is called Eat Your Heart Out, and is simply fantastic. It's like having a top-class restaurant come to you every night. At the risk of making this UK tour sound like a walk in the park, I'll give you a little sample of the menu. Tonight I started off with some absolutely delicious home-made tomato soup, followed by a selection of various salads including Caesar salad and mushroom pasta salad. Afterwards, I devoured an entire salmon dish with roasted vegetables, fit for a king. I nearly didn't have any room for the home-made rice pudding, but I forced myself, due to the fact that I would be exerting an inordinate amount of energy over the following hours playing drums.

Because I was awake really early this morning, and had a full day before I even got to Cardiff, I was overly pleased and quite surprised to find a comfortable bed in the room adjoining our dressing room at the venue. And I made very good use of it, I have to tell you. At 6.30pm I lay down on it, and promptly fell fast asleep. Udo, our tour manager, came to wake me at 7.30pm with a 'gentle nudge': he grabbed my leg, pulled it vigorously and shouted in a loud voice and with a heavy German accent, 'Get up, get up... 40 minutes 'til show time, you idiot!' I pointed out that this wasn't the nicest way to be woken, and he replied, with a wry smile, 'I'm not paid to be nice.' Actually he is very nice indeed, albeit with a very convincing sergeant major demeanour. Although he would be able to beat the England rugby team single-handedly, he's a big softy. His timing was perfect, and I awoke refreshed with 40 minutes to change, warm up and drink Red Bull.

St David's Hall in Cardiff is a magnificent venue to play, due to its intimate feel. The audience appeared to wrap around the stage, and I could clearly see the faces of nearly all of them. We entered from the side of the stage to a warm reception, which progressively became glowing hot. By the second half people were on their feet, and the concert took on its own natural momentum. The show felt like a big wave carrying people with it for two hours to a crashing finale.

After the concert we drove to a hotel in Birmingham, arrived just after midnight, and checked in. This meant that the following morning, I woke up in a hotel room in the city of the next concert, enabling me to have a proper rest before the next show. The only thing left to do is to check that I've remembered to pack my clean underwear, a toothbrush, a good book and hopefully an emergency banana.

**Postcard 40**

FOR CORRESPONDENCE

FOR ADDRESS ONLY

*Saturday*
*September 11th*
*2010*

*LG Arena,*
*National Exhibition Centre*
*(NEC), Birmingham,*
*UK*

Birmingham is the hometown of The Moody Blues, so when we play the NEC (National Exhibition Centre), or the LG Arena as it is now known, we are guaranteed not only a great turnout, but also a very enthusiastic audience to boot. Last night's concert was no exception. The first time I set foot inside the NEC, 30 years ago, was when my then-girlfriend took me to see Earth, Wind and Fire, as a surprise for my birthday. I had no idea where we were going; she just told me to drive in the direction of Birmingham, and as we pulled into the arena's car park, I had no idea who we were going to see. When I found out who the band was, I was more than elated, as they are my all-time favourites.

So impressed was I with this very pleasant ruse, and the ingenuity of this clever woman, that I married her. There were a couple of additional contributing factors, of course, but this was the real clincher. Now every time I play at the NEC Arena, I am reminded of how I walked to the side of the stage all those years ago and peered over to see the trucks and equipment, along with the band members nonchalantly walking around. Two of them were throwing an American football back and forth; it was the most exotic scene I had ever set eyes on, and I imagined myself one day being part of it.

So tonight as I walked from the dressing room towards the stage and stood in pretty much the same place that Earth, Wind and Fire did all those years ago, I experienced that physical feeling of butterflies in the stomach. It was most satisfying.

Before the show, I went for a run around a pleasant-looking lake just outside our hotel. On a day that was sunny and gorgeous, with just a tinge of autumn crispness in the air, I ran the one-mile circuit three times, scattering Canada geese every time I passed their makeshift residence, which just happened to be in the middle of my running path. I don't think the nearby fishermen were too pleased, as every time I disrupted the assembly of birds, they very noisily ran off in multiple directions, disturbing the fishermen's peace and quiet.

Back at the hotel after the concert, I chatted to some of the fans in the hotel lobby, and ended up going to the bar with John and Julie to enjoy a few of glasses of wine. John and I began reminiscing about some of the more humourous happenings that have occurred over the years, and I recounted a story of one of the very first concerts I ever played with The Moody Blues, in 1991.

We performed at the Montreux Jazz Festival, and while jazz is an important part of the festival, it has, since the 1970s, presented artists of nearly every musical style imaginable, including Pink Floyd, Led Zeppelin and Deep Purple. The Moody Blues were one of many groups to play on the night in question, and we were due to go onstage at around 10.00pm, if memory serves me right.

In a small venue, more like a club than a theatre, there were five bands playing over the course of many hours. Because of the logistics of breaking down and setting up for each act, the entire evening stretched out, and our 10.00pm slot was long gone. I didn't mind, however, as I was enjoying the rather eclectic evening's entertainment. Some time after midnight, we were called backstage to get ready for our imminent performance.

With so many bands performing that night, there seemed to be literally hundreds of people milling around. Most of them were high-profile musicians, and I recognised quite a few of them, although I couldn't put names to faces. Again this didn't really matter, as this type of high profile gig was new to me, and I was just enjoying the whole process immensely. Standing with my back against the wall in the corridor, letting everybody rush around doing their various jobs, waiting for the final pieces of the equipment jigsaw to be assembled, I noticed a man of slight stature; I gathered he was American. He was probably in his 50s or 60s, but as he was African-American, I couldn't properly discern his age. A lot of people seemed to know him, though, and his hand was being shaken by almost everyone who passed. I overheard his name to be 'Kin.'

As I was the drummer playing in the next group that was going onstage, I considered myself to be at least equal to anybody standing backstage, so I decided I would introduce myself to this cool-looking dude, whoever he was. I turned, confidently reached out my hand, and said, 'Hello, my name is Gordy Marshall; I'm the drummer with The Moody Blues, don't-you-know.' (I didn't actually say don't-you-know, but I may as well have done, with the tone I used.) He very politely smiled and simply said, 'Hello, I'm Quin.' Well, I was close.

With a sort of 'whatever' attitude, I replied, 'Quin who?' To this day, his answer still makes me cringe with the deepest embarrassment possible to a professional musician. 'Quincy Jones,' was his reply.

No one had told me Quincy Jones was going to be standing

backstage, and they certainly hadn't told me he would be introducing us. Come to think of it, it's a good job they hadn't, because he's one of my musical heroes, and I don't think I would have been able to contain myself. I have never been more star struck. My palms are sweating even as I type this. I froze, unable to speak or to let go of his hand. Eventually, after searching my brain fruitlessly for some idea of what to do next, I stammered, 'Aah...yes, of course... Mr Quin, er, I mean Jones, er, I mean Mr Quincy Jone... er, I mean... indeed... of course... how pleasant to.... to meet... er... thank you.' My mind, of course, was screaming, 'You stupid fucking idiot!'

Thankfully he didn't allow me to squirm for too long, and he asked me if I was looking forward to playing. He was pleasant, relaxed and confident in a sort of world-class musician type of way. I, on the other hand, felt like a schoolboy in front of the headmaster. With the benefit of reflection, it ended up being one of life's more interesting lessons. The band walked onstage, and with a frisson of excitement, I took my seat. I looked over to Graeme on the kit next to me; he was sitting there as cool as a cucumber. He had seen what happened, but the fact that Quincy Jones was there didn't faze him in the slightest.

Quin introduced us, then sat with the monitor guy, just six feet to my left, to watch me play. I would say I was all fingers and thumbs, except of course I was holding drumsticks. They felt like somebody else's drumsticks, and the kit felt as alien to me as a cor anglais. Thankfully, The Moody Blues, having sold millions of albums, have met nearly everyone in the business. So to them it was a regular concert and they played wonderfully as usual... and thank heavens they did, as I was a mess.

Quincy Jones left after about four tunes, hopefully because he was tired, and not, as I feared, because of my playing. But from that day on I swore I would never be intimidated at the prospect of playing in front of anyone, no matter who they were. I just hope he never turns up at a concert again to test my philosophy.

After meeting my hero that night in Montreux, John took me to the bar in our hotel for a drink and we found a jam session in full swing. With so many musicians, this type of gathering was inevitable. Eventually, and not at all reluctantly, we found ourselves up on stage as the night's resident rhythm section, playing along with a steady flow of amazing musicians from both the rock and jazz genres until the sun started to flow through the window to the bar at around six in the morning.

After remembering this story, and a few other chronicles, John, Julie and I left the bar in Birmingham at around two in the morning. We were the last to leave, and we had a long bus journey to Sheffield in the morning.

**Postcard 41**

FOR CORRESPONDENCE

FOR ADDRESS ONLY

*Sunday*
*September 12th*
*2010*

*City Hall,*
*Sheffield,*
*UK*

Serie Nr. 714-6-5

I really enjoyed socialising in the bar last night after the fantastic concert at the NEC arena, but I woke this morning with a head seemingly full of cotton wool, and in desperate need of painkillers, not to mention the bathroom. Looking out the window of my hotel room, I once more cast my eyes on the lovely lake I had so enthusiastically jogged around yesterday, and determined that I would give it a miss this morning. It had nothing to do with the amount of red wine consumed last night, honest.

Occasionally I find myself walking around my room looking for something, and forgetting what it was before I've found it. This was the case this morning, so I decided to stop looking for whatever it was I was looking for, and make a coffee with the in-room coffee machine. As I drank it, I stared at the Book of Lies, unable to take in any meaningful information. It had nothing to do with the amount of red wine consumed last night, honest.

With about an hour to go before I was due down in the lobby for the trip to Sheffield, I was standing in the bathroom with one hand inside the shower testing the temperature, dressed in a way one would expect in such a pose... when the hotel fire alarm suddenly went off very loudly in my room. Now, I can only attempt to describe what it feels like to be standing there au naturel, with a hangover most scientists would be interested in, and with one wet arm, and then to hear a fire alarm. I suppose it could have been worse: I could actually have been in the shower, but I was not. I quickly phoned down to the front desk, hoping I would be told it was a false alarm, but instead of 'Hello this is Raven, welcome to the Grand Hotel for Aging Rock Drummers, how may I help you this morning Mr Marshall?' all I heard was a woman's falsetto voice shouting 'EVACUATE... EVACUATE...' There's nothing like a little panic to put a spring into your step, and it certainly had that effect on me.

So instead of gormlessly staring into the mirror and wondering if I could get away without shaving, I was now running around the room in the altogether, making hyperventilating noises, trying to work out if I had enough time to pack my computer. The next couple of minutes entailed me pulling on jeans and boots in a most ungraceful manner, stuffing my laptop into my rucksack, and running out the door. Of course when I arrived at the lift, the sign, which read 'Do not use the lift in case of emergency,' suddenly made sense. And with an exhalation of air and a sense of complete disappointment, I made for the stairs. I was on the seventh floor.

And so it was that I found myself running down the concrete emergency staircase with astonishing clarity, wondering how my backpack could hit the back of my head and my rear-end simultaneously. I had worked myself up into a panic-led speed wobble, which eventually turned into a skilful emergency-stair-descending technique (it was quite stylish by the time I got to the bottom), so much so that I ran past the ground floor and into the basement, requiring me to come back up two flights.

By the time I emerged into broad daylight, I was in full apocalypse mode. My thick head was shouting silent questions: How are we going to make the gig in Sheffield? Are we going to make the gig in Sheffield? Will we be paid? Is everybody out? (Not necessarily in that order of course.) And finally, 'Oh dear, I left my computer power cable in the room.' I saw Norda and Julie waiting at the designated meeting point, which is always the car park. Julie was in her running gear. How does she do that? I would swear she drank as much as me.

Thankfully, it turned out to be a false alarm, and almost as soon as I was outside we were ushered back in. Uncomfortable and sweating profusely, I made my way back to my hotel room, using the lift, and continued with my shave and shampoo. Ablutions complete, in an irritable mood, I made my way downstairs again for the lobby call.

We were late getting on the bus, of course, and as soon as I sat down in my seat a headache appeared from nowhere. It was the sort of throbbing that pulsates every half second, like somebody with a foot pump inflating your head. It had nothing to do with the amount of red wine consumed last night, honest. The journey to Sheffield was a little uncomfortable to say the least, but after a couple of cheese sandwiches I was feeling better, and looking forward to the show.

I found out later that at midday, as our hotel in Birmingham was evacuated because of a fire alarm, the crew and occupants of the Sheffield City Hall were also being evacuated due to a fire alarm, just as they were setting up the equipment! A weird coincidence. Explain that to me, please.

Sheffield City Hall was designed by the architect E Vincent Harris using local Darley Dale stone, and I think it's a most beautiful building. It opened on September 22nd 1932. The Moody Blues have performed here on every UK tour since I started playing with them in 1991. It's a fabulous venue in which to play, with two balconies sweeping around to the side and overlooking the stage. It meant that I could easily look up to my left (my drum kit is set over on stage left) and eyeball the people on the first balcony. In fact if it wasn't so loud I could probably carry on a conversation about the weather or something similar.

Tonight was a fabulous show, and the band conclusively filled the room with sound, due to the sheer number of speakers we have. There is no chance of someone complaining they can't hear at one of these concerts!

The drive from Sheffield back to London was long and tiring, but arriving back home exhausted sometime in the early hours of the morning, I looked forward to a day off.

**Postcard 42**

FOR CORRESPONDENCE

FOR ADDRESS ONLY

*Monday*
*September 13th*
*2010*

*London,*
*UK*

Serie N° 714.6.8

As today was a day off, I woke late and spent the entire day in my dressing gown, moping around the house, pretending to be awake. Later I had a lovely dinner with my wife and daughters where I spoke about three words, one being 'hello,' the other two being 'good night,' and went back to bed.

Rock 'n' roll.

See you tomorrow.

**Postcard 43**

Tuesday
September 14th
2010

Apollo,
Manchester,
UK

The usual rendezvous on The Good Ship happened at midday. Graeme was full of a cold, so I left him alone at the back and sat with John and Justin further down the bus. We had run out of cheese, which was not good, as cheese sandwiches appeared to be the order of the day. We were all eating cheese sandwiches for some inexplicable reason.

My brother Robert and his lovely wife Claire were to come to the concert tonight, along with some other old friends of mine. When the show began, I saw them all sitting in the fourth row right in front of me. So in between songs, when no one was looking, I took the opportunity to surreptitiously mouth a couple of obscenities to my brother (the sort only he and I understood). He's seen me play so many times over the years that I felt I had to do something additional to entertain him.

Immediately following the show, as I didn't have long to visit with my brother, I rushed to get changed. We were driving to Newcastle after the concert, which was the next day's venue. So I quickly stripped off my stage clothes, dropped them into the laundry bag, and launched with enthusiasm into my speed-shower technique. Speed-showering is one of those touring tricks which has evolved over the years; it's a skill perfected by trial and error over many tours, and has been necessitated due to the frequent occasions when we have to leave the venue quickly in order to take off in the plane before a nighttime curfew, something which is often the case at small airports in the US.

The technique begins with covering your naked self with liquid soap before you get in the shower. You know the sort... from the little metal dispenser on the wall you would find above the sink in a municipal building. It means you don't have to spend time lathering up in the shower, and you essentially walk in and just wash the soap off. It's not ideal, of course, but it is fast and it also means you don't emit an undesirable bouquet when meeting after-show guests.

So I began the process and conclusively coated all areas in liquid soap, then, shivering, walked with an altered gait to the shower. I pulled the curtain back to find the shower cubicle was still there, as I remembered it from the previous tour, but there was no shower. None. It was missing, completely ripped out and not replaced.

So here was the dilemma: guests waiting downstairs, and me with still-sweating body covered from head to toe with liquid soap — and no way of washing it off. The only option was to have a stand-up shower using the sink. There were two taps, one freezing cold and the other, of course, offering a temperature similar to that of a freshly-boiled kettle. These were the type of taps that you press down on — like the funfair attraction where you attempt to sledgehammer the button as hard as you can, to try to make the bell ring at the top of the pole — and they differed from regular taps, in that they only offer water while your hand is pressing down on them. There was, predictably, no plug.

Curiously for a room with a sink and (no) shower, it was carpeted, and as I didn't want to get the carpet too wet, I put a towel on the floor. However, trying to successfully transport the water from the taps to my body proved most difficult. Alan popped his head around the door: 'What the hell are you doing?' he asked. I was lost for words.

After attempting cold water on my left armpit, I decided that was too unpleasant and would rather risk scalding myself. I concluded the latter option was even more disagreeable, and indeed it proved very painful, so I made the decision to use a wet towel for the remainder of the activity. Normally I would take a few minutes to cool down before showering, but as my brother and other friends were waiting downstairs I was attempting to clean up as quickly as possible. I managed to de-soap most of my body with a wet towel, and also succeeded in leaving the dressing room in a state as if I had begun to shampoo the carpet, but had abandoned the project half way through.

As I searched through my bag for clean underwear, it quickly became clear that I had forgotten to bring any. So, with a heavy sigh I spent a protracted period struggling my still-sweating body – without underwear – into jeans, and feet – without socks – into Timberland boots. I have to tell you this is most difficult. I can't remember the last time I pulled a pair of boots onto bare feet, and I think the phrase for wearing jeans this way is 'going commando.'

After what seemed like a very long time, I walked, still sweating, downstairs to meet my friends and relatives. It was simply wonderful to see Robert and Claire, and Claire put on an awfully brave face as she looked like she'd been wrestling a wet dog into the back of a car after I'd given her a bear hug (I can't help myself). After the briefest of visits we were all heading for the exit to say our goodbyes. I sat down in my seat on The Good Ship by falling backwards into it, simultaneously exhaling heavily and feeling happily knackered.

There were some particularly nice bottles of 1998 Rioja on the bus, which nobody had claimed, so it seemed like a capital idea to open one. I was sitting with John, and during the course of the journey to Newcastle he had me captivated with stories of the Beach Boys and other amazing anecdotes he's collected during his years of touring. I was treated to enthralling adventures from the 1960s and some epic descriptions of what it was like in their famous 'supergroup' period. Fascinating.

During his recounting, I poured a couple more glasses of Rioja and opened a newly purchased packet of cheese. Two hours were easily filled with entertaining stories and cliffhanging narration, followed by some deep political and religious debate. At around 1am, as we pulled into Newcastle, it dawned on me that I'd consumed an entire bottle of wine, and – apart from some cheese – hadn't eaten anything since six the previous evening. While it was a most pleasant feeling, I was under no illusion as to what type of headache awaited me in the morning.

**Postcard 44**

FOR CORRESPONDENCE

FOR ADDRESS ONLY

*Wednesday*
*September 15th*
*2010*

*City Hall,*
*Newcastle,*
*UK*

Serie N° 7114 S

I opened the heavy velvet curtains in my hotel room to find the weather bright and sunny, which was a little painful to observe as I'd woken up with a teensy-weensy bit of a hangover. Going down to the hotel restaurant, I treated myself to eggs florentine and a pot of tea, finishing off with some toast and marmalade. Breakfast is a really important part of the day for me, and today it helped me recover from my overconsumption of red wine the previous evening.

Tonight's show was at Newcastle City Hall, which is an oblong building offering a rather pleasant smell of varnished wood. It's also a very intimate venue to play. The balcony essentially overhangs the front of the stage, which, like Sheffield and Cardiff, gives the impression of being viewed at close quarters – something I'm not used to when playing with The Moody Blues. Normally my dramatic performance is aimed at the back of an arena, which makes me wonder what my often overly enthusiastic antics look like when viewed from a distance of just ten feet, and an angle of 45 degrees above me.

As the UK leg of this tour progresses, the audiences are becoming more and more animated, and tonight was no exception. My wife's parents, Alan and Audrey, came to see the show. As they had to drive home after the concert, about an hour and a quarter away, we had just one quick drink in the sumptuous bar at the hotel after the show. I then retired to my room at what is considered an early hour on the road. I was in bed reading a book before midnight.

Waking up with a clear head after a good night's sleep, I pulled back the same thick velvet curtains to expose another beautiful sunny morning, rather less painful than the one before. With such a lovely day beckoning, I decided to take a walk outdoors to blow away the cobwebs before our journey to Liverpool today. Crossing over the famous Millennium Bridge which spans the River Tyne, I noticed a sign reading, 'Newcastle City of Sport 2010.' There were some very industrious workmen constructing a four-lane running track on the other side of the river. Managing to engage a couple of security guards in conversation – I always enjoy talking to strangers – they informed me it was the Great North Run (a high-profile sporting event) this coming Sunday, and the BBC were planning a series of television and radio events to raise awareness for this annual national event. It was most interesting to see a security guard in a plastic yellow jacket talk with such enthusiasm about this local/national event. It turned out that he himself was running in the race on Sunday.

While walking along the river, now with the hotel on the opposite side, I reminisced about my day in Des Moines, Iowa, when the opening of the footbridge was celebrated. This Millennium Bridge was a lot bigger. It is sometimes referred to as the 'Blinking Eye Bridge' or the 'Winking Eye Bridge' due to its shape and its tilting method. Although the design is very similar, this one is a suspension bridge, while the bridge in Des Moines is static. From my new vantage point opposite the hotel I could see a series of further crossings in close succession, and began to wonder why I hadn't noticed the sheer number of bridges in Newcastle before. I could count six from where I was standing in clear view and they were all close to each other, probably no more than half a mile in distance. The next bridge down was the iconic Tyne Bridge, which was opened in 1928 by King George V and is still (just) the biggest along this stretch of water.

A stiff breeze blew up the river as the sun shone brightly, so I felt a significant chill on my face from the wind, but with the scorching heat of the sun on my back, my leather jacket became hot. So as I walked over another smaller suspension bridge further down the river, I had the curious experience of sweating while my hands and face were freezing. Before me was a really beautiful view of Newcastle. The quayside is a collection of new and old buildings, including the fish market and naval headquarters – old buildings dating back to the turn of the century, designed by architects from a more flamboyant age. They are now covered in netting to stop the pigeons settling on the windowsills and relieving themselves onto the patrons of the Slug and Lettuce pub below.

Arriving back at the hotel, I found I still had an hour before lobby call, so I luxuriated in the deep bath nestled in the corner of my room. My energetic job and constant travel were starting to take a toll on my body, and my tired limbs thanked me as I immersed myself into a bath of soap suds that would not look out of place in a *Carry On* movie.

With a feeling of calm and serenity, I made my way down to

the lobby to settle my breakfast bill, then walked onto the bus. We now had a four-hour journey to Liverpool, during which Graeme and I would be sitting in the large horseshoe leather sofa built into the back section of the bus, where we eventually chose a movie to help us through the afternoon.

**Postcard 45**

FOR CORRESPONDENCE     FOR ADDRESS ONLY

*Thursday*
*September 16th*
*2010*

*Philharmonic,*
*Liverpool,*
*UK*

Serial №️ 711 4 3

My brother Robert, who I mentioned in the Sheffield postcard, is a Michelin Star chef who runs his own gastro pub and restaurant and also holds the position of Head of School at Kendal College in the Lake District, where they teach the next generation of chefs. So it always gives me great pleasure to be able rub his nose... I mean, to tell him about our own travelling catering company Eat Your Heart Out. They make all the food for the band and crew on our UK tours. This is some of the best food – apart (ahem) from my wife's cooking of course – that I've ever eaten.

Incidentally, my wife really is a great cook. I was once watching her sweating away making some delicious concoction for the family and a very large group of random schoolchildren in our kitchen in Wimbledon, and I happened to say in a contemplative tone while rubbing my chin, 'You know, when I'm really rich I think I'll have my own personal chef.'

She slowly turned while holding a rather dangerous-looking carving knife and quietly replied as she waved the knife in my direction, 'Darling, you already have one.'

Meanwhile, Eat Your Heart Out also catered for *The War of the Worlds'* tour last year, so Justin and I know them really well. I have the sneaking suspicion that Justin may have had something to do with them being booked for this tour, but don't quote me on that. To give you an idea of the sort of cuisine we are treated to daily, this was the menu in Liverpool:

*Thai sweet potato soup*
*Teriyaki chicken with Chinese cabbage*
*Beansprout salad*

*Lamb shank with horseradish mash and gravy*
*Tortellini, mozzarella and basil with pesto cream*

*Caesar, tomato and artichoke salad*
*Cous cous with apricots, raisins and cashew nuts*
*Asian green noodle salad*

*Warm chocolate fondant*
*Tiramisu*
*Fruit salad*

The menu changes every day, and it's always delicious. One of the highlights of the gig is walking into the dressing room and looking for the plain sheet of A4 paper with that day's culinary options printed on it. On occasions when we've been travelling all day, and we're really hungry, I'll spend the duration of sound check trying to make my mind up between, say, garlic and herb chicken, and Indian portobello mushrooms, saag aloo and mint raita. Often I have no idea what I'm ordering but I know it will be sumptuous.

Alan has been a confirmed vegetarian since childhood and won't eat 'anything with eyes'. Recently he chose the nut roast with all the trimmings from the menu and such was its flavour, he couldn't believe it wasn't meat. Alan asked the question, 'Hey man, there's meat in here, isn't there?'

Chris, our chef, replied simply, 'No.'

'I can tell, you know... there's definitely meat in this,' continued Alan.

But Chris confidently told him the ingredients, having made it from scratch. Alan still wasn't convinced. 'I'm not so sure man, this tastes very meaty to me.'

So Chris said, 'How about I tell you I've catered for the past seven Paul McCartney tours?' Paul, of course, is a famously fastidious vegetarian.

'Aha... well, there you go.' Alan was eventually satisfied.

This brings me to the show in Liverpool (it doesn't, actually, but I had to get here somehow). Well, it was wonderful. We have never played this venue before, but the Liverpool Philharmonic is another one of those premier buildings where countless world famous performers have graced the stage. The audience surged ahead, becoming more vocal throughout the concert, and ended on a fantastic high. With eight concerts behind us, and eight in front, we were smack bang in the middle of this leg of the tour, but things began to get tough from here.

We drove from Liverpool after the concert to London, which was 230 miles. It felt like a longer journey to me and what conversation there was, was slow. If touring is a metaphor for life, then this journey could be classified as a small midlife crisis. After dropping Udo, Alan and Julie at the 'hub' hotel on the outskirts of London,

Justin, John, Norda and I climbed into a series of waiting black cars and were driven at speed along the deserted nighttime roads to our various houses in and around London. I eventually got into bed at my home around four in the morning. No red wine on this night; I may be a drummer but I'm not stupid.

As a hired musician, I have other sources of income from various other bands and shows. The Moody Blues are my priority, so I'm usually juggling other work around their tours. When one of my other clients asks me to help them out in an emergency, and I can do it, I will. You never know when any job will cease to be, so it's essential to keep as many irons in the fire as possible. It just so happens I was asked to cover a job the following day.

**Postcard 46**

FOR CORRESPONDENCE

FOR ADDRESS ONLY

*Friday*
*September 17th*
*2010*

*London,*
*UK*

Serie nº 314 4 B

So it was that I found myself sitting at a drum kit, six hours after getting back from Liverpool, for a full production rehearsal at Three Mills Studios in east London (about an hour's train journey from my house), for the touring production of *Thriller Live*, the Jacksons' musical. Three separate sessions: 10.00am to 1.00pm, 2.00pm to 6.00pm and 7.00pm to 10.00pm. After dragging myself out of bed on less than four hours' sleep, I jumped on the correct train just in time with all the regular commuters going into the city, and sat next to a couple of guys talking about their previous evening. It had been a relaxing night with their girlfriends drinking wine and watching a movie. I sat there smiling to myself, thinking how it would be nice to do that sometime.

Just to give you an idea of the sort of thing that can happen from time to time to this minstrel in London, what follows is an adventure I had earlier in the year, prior to this tour.

I was standing in the front doorway of my home as the phone rang – it was the drummer from the show *Thriller Live* in the West End of London. Not the touring version, but the resident show at the Lyric Theatre (from time to time I cover for him). His train had been cancelled, and he was going to miss the start of the show.

As I live closer to the theatre than he does, he wanted to know if I would be able to get there to the start the show – he would follow as soon as he could. The only problem was that I was just about to go out to a restaurant to celebrate my mother-in-law's 70th birthday. I was all dressed up in a clean shirt, nice white stripy trousers purchased from Zara on the recent Moody Blues US tour, and my wife and daughters were already in the car, with uncle and auntie and all.

Normally when I play in *Thriller Live* I leave about 90 minutes to get to the theatre; on this occasion I had 40 minutes before curtain up.

With the words 'the show must go on' ringing somewhere in the back of my mind, I left a bemused family sitting in the car as I ran for the train, shouting back to them 'I'll catch you up.' They think I'm mad anyway, and these sorts of events just solidify their opinion. After catching the bus from the end of my road, and arriving at Wimbledon station just in time to miss the train, I sent a text to the musical director of the show telling him I had missed the train that would have got me there on time, but that I should be there just after 7.30pm.

What followed was a frantic and rushed journey from Wimbledon to Waterloo Station, followed by me sprinting to the underground station to ride the three stops on the Bakerloo line to Piccadilly Circus. I hadn't realised the true distance between the trains until undertaking this frenzied journey. The London Underground is extremely hot in the summer, and I found myself perspiring freely and with a certain disquiet, charging past other commuters.

It was exactly 7.30pm when I emerged from Piccadilly Circus station, with several hundred yards to cover on foot before I arrived at the theatre. At this point no one in the theatre knew what my progress was. Aware that there was an entire cast waiting on stage, a full band (minus the drummer) sitting at their instruments and an audience impatiently glancing at their watches, I hastened my step. I eventually rammed through the stage door at 7.34pm.

Now, anyone who has been backstage in the 15 minutes prior to curtain up on a major musical will know it is a hive of activity. Athletic young dancers —wearing the attire only fit young people can get away with without being embarrassed — are running up and down stairs; stage crew and musicians are stamping out cigarettes at stage door and quickly walking to their various starting positions; a voice is heard over the backstage speakers saying things like, 'Act one beginners please ladies and gentlemen, this is your act one, beginners – members of the cast to the stage, and gentlemen of the orchestra to their positions please, this is your act one beginners, thank you.' It is an industrious, energetic and bustling atmosphere full of anticipation, sometimes tinged with a little stage fright.

Compare that to what greeted me: total and utter silence. There was none of the restless activity of the preshow, there was no one to be seen, not a single person anywhere, just sheer quietude. Everybody was on stage waiting to start the show, and I was the final piece of the jigsaw. The only thing left to do before I ran to the drum kit was to visit the bathroom; in my rush to leave the house, I had ignored the need to go. Now it was an immediate necessity.

Pause with me for a second while we ponder the concept of needing to micturate, but under the circumstances not being able to. Standing in the small cubicle that is the backstage loo, looking at the ceiling, legs slightly apart, left hand on the waist, while the other was... well, let's describe it like this, 'gently trying to encourage the process,' muttering through clenched teeth and with a somewhat impatient tone 'c'mon...c'mon.' All the while knowing there are over 1,000 people waiting for you. 'Now is not the time for performance anxiety Gordon,' whispered a silent voice inside my head.

After managing to squeeze out just enough to feel a little more comfortable, I turned to make my way to the stage, while simultaneously attempting to button up my fly. These new white stripy trousers from Zara, I have to tell you, have the most uniquely awkward buttoning system known to man. Normally the hole that buttons pass through (whether on trousers or a shirt) is vertical. Not on these trousers. The hole that the button goes through on these trousers is horizontal, meaning I was standing on the stairs outside the bathroom, fiddling with my trousers, but looking like I was trying to insert a suppository. With the words 'Oh, sod it' (or some similar parlance), I left my fly undone and ran to the stage.

The musical director was pacing up and down, and upon seeing me, said – I must say in a rather relaxed tone – 'We have a drummer.' Although I was sartorially ill-suited for the performance (all the other musicians were dressed in Chic black and my journey had left me looking more like someone who just survived a mining disaster), I sat down at the drum kit with a feeling of private gratification at having made it. Within 30 seconds the curtain went up and the show started.

Mike Bradley, the regular drummer came running in about 30 minutes later, looking equally tousled, having undergone an even worse journey, and we swapped over. He is a simply fabulous player, and began playing as if nothing had happened. I left quickly to find my way to the birthday party I was now late for.

When I arrived at Carluccio's restaurant – only one and half hours late – my family, consisting of aunts and uncles, grandparents, cousins, brothers-in-law, sisters-in-law, et al., all burst into a spontaneous round of applause. Having never been known to shy away from approbation, I raised my arms in Messiah-like fashion and walked through the restaurant towards the party, nodding graciously at all the tables along the way. It wasn't until I sat down at the table that one of my brothers-in-law leaned over and said 'Gordon, your flies are undone.'

**Postcard 47**

FOR CORRESPONDENCE     FOR ADDRESS ONLY

*Saturday*
*September 18th*
*2010*

*Royal Centre,*
*Nottingham,*
*UK*

Serie № 714.x.5.

There are eight shows to go before the end of the tour, and with me filling in the days off with further work, I'm beginning to feel rather drained to say the least. With hindsight, yesterday's *Thriller* session was probably a gig too far, and after the trip from Liverpool my body was feeling decidedly shaky. However, Nottingham is my hometown, and while I felt like every cell was lacking any inclination to move, with a few hours on the bus to recover I was sure I would be back to my active self by the time we arrived in Nottingham.

On the drive through the outskirts of the city, I found myself looking out of the window of the tour bus in a reminiscent mood. On my 17th birthday I'd reluctantly had to leave Nottingham to move to Blackpool with my mother and stepfather to begin a new life running a guesthouse. I was now thinking of the important people of my formative years, long gone from my life.

This was before email and mobile phones of course, so all of my school friends and music teachers from that time, along with my very first girlfriend, simply disappeared out of my life forever. I did attempt to stay in touch with everybody, which included writing to my girlfriend Karen every day for a few months, but life moves on, and a year or so later I got a job playing on a cruise ship in the Caribbean for six months. So that put paid to any continuity of correspondence.

These memories brought back bittersweet feelings as I observed all the strangely familiar landmarks from what seemed like a previous life. For a short while we travelled along the bus route to my old music school, then we passed the studio where I used to go for piano lessons with my favourite teacher, David Wilson. At a traffic light we pulled up next to the cathedral where my parents got married, and after what seemed like a very long time, the green light moved us on. I twisted the gold band on my little finger; it's the ring from that wedding, and my mother gave it to me just before she died nearly 20 years ago (tomorrow is her birthday). This was also the cathedral where my Uncle Peter was the organist and choirmaster for 30 years, after his tenure at St Paul's Cathedral in London.

It's strange how a little bit of fatigue, along with some poignant memories, can bring a lump the size of a small orange to one's throat. Realising these emotions were doing me no good at all, I promptly snapped myself out of it, and pulled my mind back to the current day. A minute later, we were pulling up outside tonight's venue – the Nottingham Royal Centre. The activity of everybody getting up, collecting bags and physically moving, assisted my recovery from the melancholy mood. Everything seemed strangely familiar, from the town to the accent of the stage doorman who looked disturbingly like my old geography teacher. He couldn't possibly be. Mr Norfolk was in his 90s when I was at school nearly 30 years ago.

Although I know this venue like the back of my hand, the

routine orange gaffer tape (a more recent familiarity) was taped to the floor with directions to the stage and dressing rooms. I played here with the school orchestra, and also when I toured with *Joseph and the Amazing Technicolor Dreamcoat*... directly after sleeping in a potting shed in Plymouth for two weeks if I remember rightly.

Just to complete the nostalgia, on the menu tonight was a roast beef dinner, with all the trimmings. So I heartily got stuck into the culinary delights of the day, ending with a warm chocolate fondant – food of champions.

Nottingham, with the River Trent running through it, was granted a city charter as part of the Diamond Jubilee celebrations of Queen Victoria in 1897. It is, of course, famously known for Robin Hood, and more recently for its lace-making and bicycle industries. My Nana, who taught me the piano from age seven, worked at the Raleigh bicycle company during the Second World War. When I first left school in 1976 I briefly had a job as a compositor printer at Boots the printers, which was then the biggest printing factory under one roof in Europe. My father used to put model ships inside bottles, and he also used to frequent what is claimed to be the oldest inn in England, Ye Olde Trip to Jerusalem. There is still a ship in a bottle, which he gave them in 1959, hanging above the bar. A true drummer's dad if ever there was one.

The concert at Nottingham – a sell-out – was magnificent. Nearly all of these UK city venues appear to be able to allow the performer to see the members of the audience clearly, something that is not part of an arena show. The fact that these venues are indoors keeps all of the enthusiastic applause and cheering at close quarters, which in turn feeds the band's motivation. So regardless of how tired I'm feeling, an energy from seemingly nowhere miraculously takes over, and all my worries of fatigue disappear. During the show when Justin introduced the backing musicians, he announced me by saying '...and from Nottingham, Gordy Marshall.' There was an extra cheer that night, as a local boy was announced.

When the show had finished and we all walked down to the front, I took a slightly over-theatrical bow. Like other nights, this is my only appearance at the front of the stage. There was a little extra cheer as all four backing musicians stepped forward to accept a moment in the spotlight. For one short moment I felt like a rock star.

On this occasion I managed to shower and change without incident, and successfully navigate my way to the back of The Good Ship. I had a sort of after-match glow: pleasantly energised but simultaneously tired, similar to the feeling you get after a winning game of football with the school team. Graeme and I settled into one of the last of *The Band Of Brothers* episodes for the journey home, a particularly violent and realistic instalment. Lying horizontally on the plush leather stretched couch, perfectly shaped for two reclining drummers, sipping huge glasses of chilled white wine, with after-show sandwiches waiting to be eaten on the table, we both agreed that it's a much easier option playing drums in a rock 'n' roll band than being a soldier in the Second World War.

Driving down the M1 in the early hours of the morning brought on another wave of weariness. And as I sat there, I wondered how I was going to manage to get through the next eight days, which would require me to play drums every day. There are a few challenges ahead before the tour ends. in particular, we have the all-important O2 Arena show coming up. Not only will there be a slew of important music industry people there, but I have about 40 friends and family coming to see me play at this prestigious venue. No pressure.

I climbed into bed at 2:30am, exhausted but unable to sleep. I lay in bed looking at the dark ceiling listening to my breathing, waiting for a suspension of consciousness; at 3.30am I gave up and took a sleeping tablet. Livin' the rock 'n' roll dream.

**Postcard 48**

FOR CORRESPONDENCE    FOR ADDRESS ONLY

Sunday
September 19th
2010

Regent Theatre.
Ipswich.
UK

If there had to be a low point somewhere in this tour, then maybe today was it. Normally I write a humorous account of things, always looking for a positive angle, and something to smile at, but of course there is no yang without yin. While most of my experiences are yang, today I'm afraid this postcard comes from the yin side of touring.

Reluctantly, I dragged myself out of bed this morning, only five hours after getting into it. It may as well have been the middle of the night, gauging by the way I was feeling, and I finished my morning rituals feeling completely exhausted. A taxi took me to the hotel meeting point, but within two minutes of sitting in the comfortable passenger seat, I fell fast asleep. The driver woke me when we arrived at the hotel with the bus waiting, and that was when I sneezed.

There is one critical rule about being on the road which probably comes before 'play fabulously.' It is simply Do Not Get Sick. If you become sick on tour, then stay away from anyone who sings. If the lead singer of a band loses his or her voice, there is no gig. If you are the one responsible for giving them the cold in the first place, you will not be popular. So this sneeze was about as welcome as a fart in a space suit (to quote Billy Connolly).

If a cold does appear, it's best to go into self-imposed solitary confinement, which is normally at the back of the bus. Although this cold didn't flourish into a fully fledged hacking cough, with associated running nose, sore throat and loss of voice, there is no knowing what this little blighter would morph into if it were to make its way to any other band member. So sitting quietly at the back, well away from everyone and wearing a white surgical mask, I wallowed in my self-pity, feeling unhappy and tired.

Soundcheck went really well, considering. I stayed clear of everyone as far as possible, and even ate dinner in my dressing room, darting into dark doorways backstage if I saw John or Justin. Before long, the process leading up to emerging on stage was underway, and with a professional smile and determined approach I took to the drum stool.

As the first set got under way, I realised very quickly that things were not proceeding as normal. I very much doubt the audience noticed of course, as everything from front of house went well. The sound was loud, crisp and punchy, and all seemed to enjoy the concert – standing ovations, the whole nine yards. However, in the name of literary honesty I have to tell you things were a little different for me.

Firstly, this was the only concert I'd done this year with a chill in the air, and due to the fact that the venue in Ipswich is small, all the flight cases were stored outside in the open. It looked a little like someone was moving house, with the assistance of a lot of awfully enthusiastic helpers.

Whether it was fatigue or not I don't know, but I found myself losing my concentration during the show. As I was banging away trying to enjoy the atmosphere, I'd start to wonder, 'Is this the first verse or the second?' followed by a series of musical near-misses.

Of course the illusion of musical proficiency had to continue, so these occasional setbacks can normally be circumvented by toughing it out and throwing yourself into the performance even more. They can often end up being some of the best shows due to their unpredictability. But tonight was a struggle for me. Some nights the drums seem to just play themselves, and on other occasions, like tonight, I'm seemingly required to prise every single note out of the instrument against its better judgment. This, along with the accumulated fatigue from constant travel, had proven to be a psychological dip in the tour.

I described The Good Ship Everything in the US as being like a submarine, but the bus in the UK, which I haven't much mentioned, would be the sailboat above it. Making a cup of tea in this moving metal tube really is like making tea at sea. Pouring boiling water from the kettle requires you to stand with your legs firmly apart and hips wedged up against the work surface for stability. With a cup over the sink in one hand, and a kettle in the other, this martial arts-type stance ensures that any 'spare' boiling water goes into the sink.

We also have the cruelly unsympathetic roads and traffic jams associated with travel in the UK. If we were on a plane, I would describe it as taking a series of long haul flights with significant and continuous turbulence.

I have read a lot about the law of attraction, and while I would never claim to be an expert on the topic, I can't help but feel that most people will have experienced something similar in their daily life, either at work or at home. Normally, things just go according to plan, and the more you get on a roll the better everything becomes.

Then something happens to upset the emotional apple cart, and, all of a sudden, life appears to be heading in the wrong direction. It's as if our minds control the outer world, and when we begin to feel as if everything is going wrong, the universe follows our thought process to the letter. On the bus back home tonight I entered into a debate with myself about the whole topic, and emerged none the wiser.

And so I sit here in my kitchen at 3.00am, contemplating tomorrow's awakening, wondering if I will have shaken off this feeling and be happy to open my eyes to another day, or if will I continue with my melancholy mindset.

My children will come into the bedroom to kiss me goodbye as I sleep, before they go off to school; my dog Harley will undoubtedly be wagging her tail when I arise; and my wife will have a cup of hot tea ready as I shuffle into the kitchen around 11.00am, so I stand a very good chance of shifting the mood to a more positive frame of mind. This is one benefit of being on tour and at home at the same time, and therefore tomorrow's gig in Oxford may provide the emotional shift I crave. The amazing thing is, as long as the music is authentic, the audiences do not seem to discern any difference in my mood, thank heavens.

I'm off to bed.

**Postcard 49**

FOR CORRESPONDENCE

FOR ADDRESS ONLY

*Monday*
*September 20th*
*2010*

*Apollo,*
*Oxford,*
*UK*

Serie Nº 714-C.R.

Today I continued with my self-imposed separation from the band and decided to drive to Oxford in my own car, just in case the cold developed into something more serious. As it happened, it didn't advance into anything of substance, and although my fatigue had not been conquered, the cold was holding back.

Apart from a sell-out gig at the Oxford Apollo, which was simply amazing, nothing of any consequence happened today. So instead I will tell you about the circumstances which led to me sitting on the film set of the Hollywood movie, *Ocean's Eleven*. I'm referring of course to the 2001 remake of the 1960 Rat Pack caper of the same name, which was filmed in Las Vegas at the same time The Moody Blues were performing.

During the 1990s and into the noughties, The Moody Blues played at Caesar's Palace in Las Vegas every year. We used to play for two weeks in the spring, and then another two weeks in the autumn. In total, for one month of every year we lived in the amazing and truly 24-hour city of Las Vegas. In fact The Moody Blues became so associated with Las Vegas that when *The Simpsons* based one of their episodes there, they included the band in the story. John, Justin, Graeme and Ray went to *The Simpsons'* recording studios to record their voices for the show, and recently my teenage daughter, who is studying French at school, was watching *The Simpsons* in French as part of her lesson (it's comforting to know her education is in good hands) and it was that very episode which her class saw.

One Saturday night in the main room at Caesar's Palace, towards the end of a concert, I saw a man I did not recognise standing at the side of the stage. This is a no-go area during a performance for anybody not directly involved in the show, so I thought it a little unusual that this large, besuited, middle-aged man with greying hair was standing next to the monitor desk. He wore a broad smile, and was dancing.

After the show, he followed Graeme and I into the dressing room – another area reserved exclusively for people involved in the show, especially immediately after a performance. It was then I was introduced to Jerry Weintraub. The reason he was able to wander into the inner sanctum so easily is because, in addition to managing Elvis Presley, Led Zeppelin, the Carpenters, Frank Sinatra and Neil Diamond, he used to manage The Moody Blues. As Graeme and I were getting changed, he was chatting about his time managing the band, which of course was fascinating, as it was during their 'supergroup' period. Wanting to be involved in the conversation, I posed a question – 'What are you doing now?'

'Well, I don't manage bands any more, but I'm making a movie at the Bellagio Casino,' he replied.

Now everyone in either LA or Vegas is 'making a movie' or 'involved in a project,' and I concluded – rather cruelly – that as he wasn't managing bands anymore, that he was a bit of a has-been.

'That sounds interesting,' I said in a rather uninterested tone. 'Who's in it then?'

'George Clooney, Brad Pitt, Matt Damon, Andy Garcia, Julia Roberts...' he said.

Well, you could have knocked me over with a feather, quite frankly. It was one of those moments in life when I couldn't quite believe my ears; he had started his reply when I had one leg out of my trousers, and he stunned me into a statue-like stance in that very position.

The only intelligent response I could think of was 'Wow.'

After he had chatted with John and Justin in their dressing rooms, he popped his head around the door once more and said, 'We're shooting a big scene tomorrow at 10.00am, why don't you come over to watch it? Just find one of the runners, and ask for me.' Well, there was an offer I could not refuse. I just had to work out the logistics.

We normally started our set at about 10.10pm, and played for 90 minutes, which meant by the time our show finished and I had showered and changed, it would be after midnight. Add to that the surge of adrenaline flowing through my veins after playing a rock show, and the fact that Las Vegas had no shortage of activities throughout the night, and bedtime would usually be somewhere in the region of stupid o'clock. Being awake at 10.00am in Las Vegas normally meant a late night out wasn't yet over. Tonight, though, I determined to go straight to bed in order to accept this terribly exciting invitation.

My room in Las Vegas was home to a round four-poster bed, with a mirror above it the same size and shape as the bed. Along with this unique and interesting berth were other distractions not found in my semi-detached house in Wimbledon: a large, circular bath so big it was advisable to arrange any ablutions at least two days prior, to allow enough time to fill the tub, and a pink chaise longue with leopardskin cushions. Goodness only knows what sort of things the management was expecting me to get up to.

So when the alarm went off in the morning – something I definitely was not used to in Las Vegas – I awoke on my back and caught sight of myself in the mirror above, and for a split second I thought a perverted intruder had sneaked into in the room. I followed this disturbing experience with a few laps of backstroke in my bathtub using yesterday's bathwater, and eventually made my way downstairs and out into daylight. Now there is a novelty – Las Vegas in daylight.

I have to say I was already in pretty high spirits at the prospect of seeing the set of a Hollywood movie, and I navigated the immensely complicated walkways and escalators to the Bellagio Hotel opposite Caesar's Palace and made my way into the casino. It dawned on me that I had no idea where to go, as it's such a huge complex, so I made my way to the main casino. I needn't have worried. The filming of this movie had taken over a large part of the casino floor, and what would normally be filled with hopeful gamblers at slot machines was now a roped-off film set, with a huge standing audience of ten people deep.

Gingerly, I pushed my way through the crowd, apologising in my best English accent with the words 'Excuse me' and 'I'm so sorry, can I just... thank you,' all the while squeezing through the throng. Eventually I got to the rope, which didn't seem to offer much in the way of security, but everybody was respectful enough to realise this was a definite line of demarcation.

Thankfully, very close to my vantage point I spotted an eager, spectacled and intelligent looking young woman carrying a clipboard, who was clearly meant to be on the other side of the rope. I called her over, again in my best English accent, and tried to whisper to her that I was a guest of Jerry Weintraub, and could I please be taken to him. She looked at me as if I had bad breath, but at least she did take my name. Two minutes later she returned and asked me to follow her, and within a matter of seconds I was sitting next to Jerry Weintraub, the producer of *Ocean's Eleven*, on the film set... it was exhilarating.

I had to remind him who I was, because although he had managed The Moody Blues, I was not playing with them at that time, and he had only met me for 15 minutes the previous night. I could see this was a guy with a lot on his plate. Once he had remembered who I was, he was charm itself, and started to describe to me what they were about to film, which was a scene where Brad Pitt walks across the casino floor and a fight breaks out.

As Jerry was explaining this to me, Brad Pitt walked over. They embraced like two long-lost friends, and I was beginning to feel decidedly out of place. After what seemed like a very short conversation between the two of them, the shooting of the scene began. Jerry was watching the action on a small TV screen where he and I were sitting, and the director shouted, 'Action!' Brad Pitt walked across the set as directed, with the sort of confidence and authority most people dream of, looking every bit the Hollywood film star, and all mayhem broke loose with the actors onset, as planned.

I was amazed that the hundreds of people standing behind the rope just a few feet away were deathly silent during the take. A true mark of respect, I thought. Then Brad Pitt turned around and walked back to where Jerry and I were sitting. There was a chair just to the right of me, and Brad sat in it. Jerry briefly introduced me, and Brad, who was now sitting no more than six inches away, said 'Hello.' So there I was, Jerry Weintraub sitting on my left, and Brad Pitt sitting on my right, on the set of *Ocean's Eleven*.

Things like this happen when you tour with The Moody Blues: things so out of the ordinary that I find I have to issue a good pinch to my person just to make sure I am truly there.

It would be really nice to continue the story by telling you Brad and I became bosom buddies, and he's invited me to act with him in his next movie. Alas, after the briefest of chats he was once more employed in the much more important role of acting. I sat there (mostly in silence) for about an hour and a half, trying not to get in the way, but simply enjoying the whole procedure. After I had outstayed my welcome by maybe an hour and 25 minutes, I thanked Jerry Weintraub profusely, telling him I had some important business to take care of, and left the set.

Climbing under the rope through the crowd of spectators on the way out was a completely different experience to trying to get in. I felt like one of the Israelites crossing the Red Sea, with people standing aside to let me through. It dawned on me that after seeing me sitting between these two very famous people, they thought I was somebody important to the movie. Little did they know that I'm just a drummer in a rock 'n' roll band. Here I was living the life of a rock star, without actually being one.

The glorious sunshine accompanied me back to my residence at Caesar's Palace, and I wandered on through the seemingly endless corridors towards my splendorous room in a state of surrealism. It wasn't until I lay down on the bed, and I was again confronted with the reality of my reflection from the mirror above, that I came back down to earth.

**Postcard 50**

FOR CORRESPONDENCE    FOR ADDRESS ONLY

Tuesday
September 21st
2010

London,
UK

At this stage in the tour, it is beginning to feel exactly like the movie *Groundhog Day*. Of course each of the concerts in themselves are wonderful to play, but the travel is exactly the same – long bus journey to venue, long bus journey from venue – and I can feel an increasing level of fatigue overtake me.

This means that today's diary entry, which was supposed to be a day off from the tour, was indeed a *Groundhog Day*. A few months ago, with an overly optimistic opinion of my capabilities and thinking I could fit a gig in around this time, I accepted another engagement in *Thriller Live* at the Lyric Theatre, and tonight I did indeed play another show. Halfway through *Don't Stop 'Til You Get Enough* from the *Off The Wall* album, I promised myself I would never again accept additional work during a tour. About two songs later we launched into *Workin' Day and Night* from the same album, and at this point my legs were starting to wobble beneath me. This was the confirming factor for me that I will not be working day and night like this ever again.

Even though most of the daylight hours had seen me in bed, horizontal and relaxed, the level at which I was pushing myself had outstripped the good-night's-sleep remedy. What was really needed was one or two weeks' complete rest from playing, but I still had another couple of weeks before that scenario would present itself. In the meantime it was a question of keeping my head down, and battling through.

So, here I sit at home in the middle of the night, with the final five concerts of this Moody Blues tour ahead, and a further six Thriller gigs slotted around them over the next 12 days. If I can make Amsterdam without falling over I will be very happy, as after that I can finally relax.

Let us rewind this journal to the weeks of August, in-between the two legs of this tour. I played a one-off engagement for the *Thriller Live* touring show. It was an outdoor show on the lawn of a beautiful stately home called Audley End, just outside London. The regular drummer needed to be somewhere else and I was dispatched to cover this one show.

It was a fabulous day, and included me playing drums on a tour, but I realised what a contrast it was to touring with The Moody Blues. On this Moody Blues tour, I am, at age 50, the youngest guy in the band by comparison. Youngest chronologically, anyway: Graeme still packs a punch behind the kit, and is out energetically travelling the world on a regular basis. I'm sure many people feel old by comparison when they see him thrashing away on the drums, and dancing around the stage as if he were 30 years younger. But on *Thriller Live*, I found myself feeling, shall we say, 'mature.' The *Thriller Live* touring production has the same choreographer, director and musical coordinator as the West End production and is an almost exact replica. These types of touring productions are often populated with younger musicians who are better suited to being away from home for anything up to a year at a time. This one tours around the world (they have recently just got back from ten days in China and are currently in South Africa).

My directions on the day were to meet the *Thriller* tour bus at midday at Euston station, and along with the entire cast and rest of the band we were to be driven to Audley End. On what turned out to be a gloriously sunny day, we set off with the spirits of kids on a high school outing. It was when I was chatting with the band and cast that I realised I was the only one on the bus (with the exception of maybe the driver) who was in his 50s. And with the exception of the bass player, there was no one in their 40s either. Ok...now you come to mention it, there was no one on the bus who was even in their 30s. The musical director did tell me he was 29 (because I asked him). I was beginning to feel a little like an old-timer amongst this group of seriously hip-looking kids, if only because they appeared to be treating me to a little more respect than I am used to: standing up to let me sit down, offering a hand when stepping from the bus, asking if there was anything they could get for me, that sort of thing.

This was all very well and good, and if this is what awaits me in my dotage then all I can say is 'bring it on,' but what I was not expecting was the sheer level of musicianship and professionalism offered by these children (you can say that sort of thing when you get to my age). When they began to warm up before the soundcheck, it became clear I was in the company of some seriously schooled musicians, but when they commenced playing for real, it was all I could do to not shout 'Wow!' I honestly do not remember being that good at that age. It's one thing to be playing in a major musical in London or New York; you sort of expect to be blown away. It's another thing altogether to be blown away by kids who aren't old enough to date your teenage daughters.

Of course the usual daily trivial obstacles presented themselves. The driver backed the bus into the hedgerow while attempting to turn the vehicle from the single lane road into the grounds, choking off the engine and blocking traffic in both directions. This is an issue when you have thousands of spectators all trying to enter through the same gate. It necessitated all the cast and band exiting the bus and walking through the car park, entering the venue from the back of the lawn where the audience was sitting. We weren't allowed in because we didn't have tickets, so we had to wait for the company manager to walk several hundred yards from the stage to the entrance, to talk to the security guard as if he were a schoolboy, in order for him understand the group of 30 or so thespians holding guitars and suit bags, were actually performers.

Apart from that, the whole endeavour was an utter joy with which to be involved. Playing to several thousand enthusiastic audience members soaking up sunshine and alcohol in equal measure proved the perfect mix of work and play.

I recognised one of the dancers as being someone I had worked with nearly a year before, and he recognised me, although neither of us could remember one another's name. He had been busy touring the world the previous year with the show; he was a really nice chap, and his life sounded very exciting. When he asked me what I had been doing, I (trying to stifle a little self-congratulatory smile) nonchalantly replied,

'Well, I've just come off an American tour with The Moody Blues.' He looked at me with a fixed smile, as if still waiting for an answer. 'You know? The Moody Blues?'

It dawned on me that this charming and very respectful 18 year old, who had offered me his hand as I alighted the bus, might have never heard the name.

'Ah man.... I luuurve the Blues,' he said as he looked at his watch using peripheral vision. I could tell his interest only went so far, and I didn't blame him.

'You've heard... of The Moody Blues?' I uttered with the same surprised inflection Chief inspector Dreyfus uses in *The Pink Panther* when he says, 'Clouseau... is alive?'

'Well er, no... I've never heard of them, but I love the blues.'
I decided it was best to leave it at that, and I can imagine him asking the other 18 year old dancers, 'Did you know that nice old guy on drums plays in a blues band?'

Nevertheless, it was a fabulous gig, and I was happy to sit there as a complete unknown and be part of the touring version of *Thriller Live* for one night.

**Postcard 51**

FOR CORRESPONDENCE

FOR ADDRESS ONLY

*Wednesday
September 22nd
2010*

*Hippodrome,
Bristol,
UK*

This morning things were a lot brighter. The sun was out, I'd had a good night's sleep, and I was looking forward to playing in one of my favourite cities: Bristol. My real-life *Groundhog Day* began with the same taxi driver picking me up to escort me to the meeting point, and within 30 minutes I found myself sitting on the bus with a cup of tea and a cheese sandwich, laughing hysterically with Norda, Julie, Alan and Graeme over a joke about an apprentice lion tamer. If you ever see me in person ask me about it and I'll tell it to you. The bus pulled away for our Bristol hit and run, me with tears streaming down my face, unable to contain my hyena-esque guffawing.

Once we hit the M4 travelling west, the going was smooth, and Graeme and I spent hours trying to decide which movie to watch.

We devised a system of auditioning movie titles: when we didn't know anything about a given movie we started by watching the first five or ten minutes of it, and if one of us gave it the thumbs down, we simply pressed 'stop' and moved to the next one. The bus entertainment system had a number of hard drives containing thousands of movies, TV shows, documentaries, etc., so our afternoon consisted of over four hours of watching the first few minutes of dozens of movies. It's the downside of having so many options: you can guarantee that if we had just three films to choose from we would have watched one of them to the end.

Bristol Hippodrome was the very first major venue I played in the UK, during the production of *Joseph* that Andy and I were involved with all those years ago. Pulling up to the theatre once more proved to be a rather emotive experience, with the distinct memory of stage fright, and this was before I had even set foot inside the theatre. The catalyst for this emotion was a beautiful and imposing structure, designed by Frank Matcham, and officially opened in December 1912. It's now a Grade II listed building. The theatre used to house a huge water tank (it could hold over 10,000 gallons) at the front of the stage, with an accompanying protective glass screen. The tank was taken out at some point; I imagine the actors were getting wet.

This formidable auditorium, which survived the Second World War, also has an ornate central dome that can be popped open when necessary, like a city gent doffing his hat. However, now the theatre is fully air-conditioned, it's rarely opened. Considering it's one of the biggest stages outside of London, and not only accommodates all the major travelling musicals but was also the venue chosen for the British premiere of *Guys and Dolls* in 1961, it's in a very difficult position to get to. Not only is there not much room for trucks and buses to park, but it's very difficult to get any large vehicle anywhere close to the stage door. As a consequence there was no catering tonight. There was simply nowhere to cook, or serve food for 30 hungry crew and band members.

So this afternoon after the soundcheck, I ventured out into the real world for dinner. First, though, I went for a little run to check out Bristol, since it had been quite a few years since I passed through. Leaving the stage door and into the lane at the side of the theatre,

I ran down Denmark Street and onto the main road – Anchor Road – and down towards the harbour just a few hundred yards away. Running along Canon's Road with the water to my left, I passed the Imax theatre and carried on into a pedestrian area, where I was nearly frightened to death by a huge sculpture of an insect.

Continuing to the Millennium Square Ferry Landing, I began to feel a little cold and tired, and given the fact that I'd been feeling under the weather for the past few days I decided it might be a good idea to return to the warmth of the theatre. I noticed a sign saying 'The UK Bungee Club,' and wondered how much money I would have to be given to do that now. Deciding it would be somewhere around the same amount of air miles I currently own, I turned on my heel and made my way back to the venue.

Unfortunately the available options for pre-show fare did not look all that appetising. I scanned the road as I returned, looking for restaurants. Once I was back in the small side road next to the theatre, there were a limited number of options. None of them were particularly inspiring; Bombay Boulevard was next to Floyd's Fast Food, two doors further on was The Bunch Of Grapes pub which I have a particular drunken memory of, and Rendezvous fish and chip shop was next to that. I opted for a small Italian restaurant, where a bowl of pasta with pesto was the accompaniment to my latest Bill Bryson book. Eat Your Heart Out had really spoiled me.

With 15 minutes to doors opening, I wandered onto the stage to have a peek at where we would be playing later, and to take a look at the empty room, all set up and waiting to be kicked into life. The minutes before people walk into any venue are the most peaceful; it's like a church on a Monday morning. As I visually scanned the hall contemplating the silence, a chap quietly came up behind me and said, 'It's really nice, isn't it?'

Turning around I saw a man about my age; he was obviously one of the local crew working at the theatre, dressed in black jeans and a black shirt. His grey curly hair fell onto his shoulders, and his goatee suggested an alternative lifestyle. 'Indeed it is,' I said. 'I played here 30 years ago with *Joseph*.'

'What? The Bill Kenwright production, with David Steadman as the musical director?' he replied with some surprise.

'Yes, that's the one,' I said, with instant recognition.

'Well, that was my first job, and I've been here ever since,' he replied with animation.

This was such a coincidence that it instantly put me in mind of something. 'Hey, you're not Pete, the one that Andy and I got really drunk with at the Bunch of Grapes, are you?' I asked enthusiastically. After a momentary pause he said 'No,' and with a confused look, 'That wasn't me.'

'Oh OK then,' I murmured as I wandered offstage, 'Just checking.' Not one of my best anecdotes, I will admit, but it is true.

The concert tonight was simply stunning, with a full house, a band on top form, and an overly enthusiastic audience. The show flew by in a haze of applause and approbation. We are now officially in the final stretch of the tour, and Ipswich notwithstanding, each gig is gaining momentum. We were soon onto the bus back to London, and Graeme and I continued our fruitless search for something interesting to watch on our personal in-bus theatre.

**Postcard 52**

FOR CORRESPONDENCE

FOR ADDRESS ONLY

Thursday
September 23rd
2010

BIC (Bournemouth
International Centre).
Bournemouth.
UK

One of the better perks of being a musician (apart from being able to sleep during the day) is visiting places you wouldn't normally go to on a regular basis. So when I find myself in, say, a remote airport in the American Midwest, and it's familiar to the degree that I can point a stranger from a foreign land to the nearest bathroom, it brings about a distinct feeling of déjà vu.

Bournemouth is a place where I encounter this experience in bucketloads. Although I've never lived there, or spent any extended time there, I have simply lost count of the amount of times I have performed in this beautiful Dorset town over the years. The Bournemouth International Centre (BIC), along with many other venues we've played, is close to the water's edge. Having played here with almost every band or show I've been involved in for the past 30 years, I know it like the back of my hand.

As we approached the venue, the sea came into view from the tour bus and I found myself experiencing a childlike twinge of excitement, but no sooner had the seascape appeared than it disappeared. The Good Ship *Nearly* Everything pulled into the underground car park of the BIC, next to the hidden stage door. We all filed into the building and found our respective dressing rooms, and I immediately walked back out of the venue, to fill the hour before soundcheck with a hearty walk along the beach.

The BIC is set up on a cliff above the sea and offers a remarkable view of the Channel. Leading down to the beach are a series of very steep stone steps, which require the agility of a mountain goat to navigate. Three different people passed me on the way up, as I walked down, each in turn taking the opportunity to stop for a breather and commenting on how difficult the climb was. Eventually I arrived at beach level and walked along West Undercliff Promenade. Then, removing my Timberlands and socks, I walked onto the sand and out to the water.

Normally, I love sand. Nothing pleases me more than lying on a warm beach somewhere and occasionally getting up for a dip in the sea. Ideally this setting would be Florida, under a palm tree, in the late morning sometime in June. Unfortunately I am in Bournemouth in the late afternoon in September. With my jeans rolled up to my knees, holding my boots in my hand and not realising how cold the sea would be, I walked to the edge of the water and allowed the tiny waves to lap over my feet. The sensation was like an electric shock. It was such a chilly surprise I had to hold back feelings of nausea. I could see people swimming in the sea, for goodness sake. I imagined they had either signed up for one of those alternative health therapies where you willingly agree to undertake torturous activities, or they had taken leave of their senses.

Walking back along the cold sand, I looked like someone attempting to serenely walk over hot coals and failing. I was experiencing a pain similar to a migraine, but in my feet. Stumbling onto the paved promenade, I quickly tried to rid my feet of the cold wet sand stuck between my toes, by hitting them with my socks.

I've never understood this technique until now, but now I realise one will try any fruitless exercise when faced with this type of discomfort. With an imminent soundcheck looming, I made my way back up the stone stairs, stopping to chat to anyone coming down, just to let them know what they were in for.

Once back in the comfort of the BIC I was able to get a proper towel in an attempt to rid myself of the seemingly endless amounts of sand still stuck to my feet. I changed into sneakers for the sound check, and we played through our normal miniature set for Steve, our front of house soundman. After all this activity, I was positively starving, so quickly made my way to catering for the evening's meal. Even as I sat there devouring a lovely vegetarian lasagne, I could still feel sand between my toes.

Once again, tonight's concert did not disappoint the fans or the band. However, the room at the BIC felt as if it was the wrong way round, and instead of playing at the end of the hall, it sort of felt like we were down one side of it. This meant people were way off to the extreme left and right. Nevertheless, the show came out in the opening round with the usual heavy punches, and by half-time the audience were on their feet willing us to win. By the end it was a knockout, and even though I was feeling totally exhausted, we all walked off stage knowing it was a resounding success.

Shortly afterwards, as the water from the lovely hot shower in the dressing room washed the soap off my body, I saw more sand around my feet and considered it with a feeling of victory, knowing that after this conclusive dousing those annoying grains would not blight me any longer.

On the bus I opened a really nice bottle of Chardonnay and handed out glasses to almost everyone on board, but instead of lounging in the back watching small portions of eclectic movies, I sat with Graeme, sipping wine and discussing some of the more interesting flights we've had over the years. One particular flight popped into both our heads, from back when the Moodies hired a private plane to get to a couple of venues that were distant from each other. The plane, apparently owned by Tom Hanks, was an absolutely gorgeous vehicle: brand new with white interior, big cream leather captain's chairs, and gold coloured fittings. The airhostess had been asked to serve spare ribs for the flight. Soon after take off we were cruising at 40,000 feet over New Mexico in a clear blue sky, delicately picking ribs with red sauce off the passing platter onto our little plates. It felt like we were stationary, such were the benign flying conditions. With the gentle hum of the engines, and the civilized method of transport, everyone was relaxed.

Suddenly and without any prior warning, the plane violently tilted to starboard, sending everyone into an arms-in-the-air-position in an attempt to stop plates of spare rib and cups of coffee spilling on to the thick carpet. It was over as quickly as it began, and we all collectively held a facial expression of surprise, apart from me. I was going through a particularly decisive hate period of a love/hate relationship with flying. I'm fine now, but at the time things like this frightened the living daylights out of me.

No sooner had the first deviation from the original flight path occurred than it happened again. As far as I was concerned in that moment, this was it. I honestly thought that the plane had turned over. Of course I'm sure it didn't, but any ideas of preventing food and drink from leaving their containers were instantly gone.

The air hostess held the roof of the plane in a vain attempt to stay on her feet, while liquid went into the air and covered the white ceiling, followed swiftly by rib sauce. Seconds before, my only view had been of a clear blue sky, but now the window was filled with what looked like a giant Google map, as the side of the plane toyed with idea of taking a closer look at the ground. The engine tone increased by an octave, and the force of pulling out of the unfortunate manoeuvre made any previous rollercoaster ride feel like a stroll in the park. As I yelled 'Fuck, fuck, fuck, fuck, ffffuck' (I always wondered what my last words were going to be), the plane pulled up and regained its poise.

We continued to our destination of Albuquerque, leaving the plane as if a rock band had just been aboard – the place was trashed. The only problem being that that day was a hit and run, and we were due to fly on the same plane to another destination after the gig. I am pleased to report that the second flight of the day was much less eventful.

Back to the present day. The Good Ship Nearly Everything arrived safely from Bournemouth and dropped me off at home, and in the early hours of the morning and in a darkened house I silently changed into pyjamas, trying not to wake anyone. The following morning, my wife wakened me with a cup of tea, and said, 'Do you know, it's really weird. There's sand all over the floor.'

**Postcard 53**

FOR CORRESPONDENCE · FOR ADDRESS ONLY

*Friday*
*September 24th*
*2010*

*London,*
*UK*

After a few hours' sleep, I hesitatingly tiptoed downstairs holding an empty teacup, feeling utterly spent. My first job this morning was taking out the rubbish. My neighbour (remember him?) passed me as I was outside in my dressing gown.

'It's all right for some, lounging around in pyjamas all day,' he said without breaking step. Unfortunately he wasn't close enough for me to hit him.

Today's postcard is going to be a short one. Put simply, I'm so tired I can hardly think, and I'm playing *Thriller* tonight. So I intend to spend the day in my dressing gown and only change into outdoor clothes when it's required that I leave the house.

I heard it once said that the definition of hell is 'having to do something you love all the time', and apart from one day off 11 days ago, tonight will be the 26th night in a row that I will have played the drums. In my sleep-deprived, exhausted state, it certainly feels like a mini-hell at the moment. These swinging emotions are par for the course on tour, by the way. So don't be alarmed if you think I'm dangerously oscillating between depression and elation: there is nothing wrong with me that a weekend off won't put right.

But tomorrow is the Big Day, so I'm off to get some rest. See you tomorrow.

**Postcard 54**

FOR CORRESPONDENCE · FOR ADDRESS ONLY

*Saturday*
*September 25th*
*2010*

*O2 Arena,*
*London,*
*UK*

### 1.30pm

Here it is: the London O2 Arena, the high point of the tour. It seems just days since we started this UK leg, but also the longest time since I started writing this diary back in June. I'm making an entry before we play today, so this postcard will have two sections: before the gig and after.

I for one am really looking forward to playing tonight. I love playing at the O2 Arena, with its sense of occasion, and its global significance as a venue. It really garners an 'I've made it' feeling, although today of all days, I've just had a significant amount of work cancelled in the New Year and I will no doubt be reflecting with irony, how I will fill the economic gap – while sitting on one of the biggest stages in the world.

I'm feeling uncharacteristically nervous. It's weird, as I've played larger venues than the O2, and to bigger audiences. It may be due to the fact that lots of people I know will be there: all my family, many good friends and neighbours, even the head teacher of my daughter's school.

It's just one hour before I leave to meet the tour bus, so I will try to eat some lunch, although I appear to have lost my appetite. It's been replaced with an almost continuous and irresistible desire to visit the bathroom.

### After the show

Well, I was expecting it to be fantastic, and so it proved to be. Walking onto the stage at the O2 with The Moody Blues was everything I thought it would be. Electrifying and thrilling emotions surged through my body as I walked up the steps at the side of the stage and viewed the panorama before me. My earlier nerves had been conquered, and in their place was a flow of what felt like pure adrenalin, which took some concentration to overcome during the first few songs.

The sheer enormousness of the O2 and the view when first walking inside the building give the impression of being inside a giant aeroplane hanger. It's the stage that gives away the size – it looks so much smaller from the opposite end of the room in comparison to other venues. The larger venues in America, which we play on a regular basis, are nearly always outdoors, so the perspective is completely different. Add to that the fact that the O2 is an internationally important venue, and that it's essentially in my backyard, gives it all the more significance.

Thankfully, our trusty orange gaffer tape, with directions written on them – 'Moody Blues, this way'; 'Singers, this way'; 'Production, that way'; 'Catering, over there'; etc. – directed us all effortlessly through the corridors.

The soundcheck proved to be most enjoyable, due to some additional speakers imported especially for this concert. The sound was huge, even with in-ear monitors supposedly cutting off ambient noise; I could just feel the depth of the music. Every bass drum hit was like a small explosion, every crack of the snare felt like shooting a gun, the grooves were deeper, heavier, and had additional dimension. I love playing small venues, but I adore playing these big arenas.

As the set began, the audience seemed enthralled, and it wasn't long before they were on their feet. With the electric sensation of playing on stage, the utter thrill of performing came to the fore. At times like this it is an out of body experience, where everything seems to be happening around you; it's like being a spectator at your own gig. Nothing was a problem, nothing mattered, a total suspension of reality for this short period in life. The release of endorphins into the system guarantees a pain-free high with no downside. I looked over to Graeme sitting to my right, and without saying anything, he gave me a look that said, 'Yes, I know.'

I've been doing this for 20 years now with The Moody Blues; Graeme of course has been doing this for 45 years, since the beginning. It really has to be one of the best jobs in the world. On that very point, a few years ago a film company produced a programme called *The Top Ten Best Jobs in the World*, and The Moody Blues were filmed for it while they were on tour. The job of rock star was apparently considered pretty much up there at the top of the list. However, you may be interested to know that it came in second to fashion photographer. Apparently, photographing beautiful women in bikinis (or less) on tropical beaches is considered a more preferable job.

After the concert, my wife and daughters briefly came backstage, but as they had to be up for school the next day, I decided not to wait for The Good Ship Nearly to take us home.

We left with the audience and travelled on the Underground back home. We arrived back at Wimbledon station at 11 that evening, and waited for the number 163 bus back to our house. After I had made a big jug of hot chocolate for everyone, I lay in bed, with the combined feelings of elation and utter exhaustion. Rock 'n' roll.

**Postcard 55**

FOR CORRESPONDENCE

FOR ADDRESS ONLY

Sunday
September 26th
2010

London,
UK

In theory this was a day off, but it actually wasn't. I had another gig in *Thriller* at the Lyric Theatre. Thus it was that I found myself walking once more to the bus stop at the end of my road to catch the 163 (*Groundhog Day* Express) into Wimbledon town, followed by the journey on the underground to the Lyric Theatre. The music business frequently offers a 'feast or famine' scenario, and as this was a feast of musical employment, I seemed to be cramming two days' worth of work into every one. My mind was scrambled and my body aching. It felt as though my brain was floating somewhere above me: connected by a piece of string like a balloon, but not part of the action below.

The day passed as if in a fog, going through the routine of washing, dressing and eating, and having to drag myself through every activity in the most painful fashion. As the end of this Moody Blues tour appeared on the horizon, my battle with fatigue was getting worse.

I find it quite remarkable that the human body is capable of pushing itself much further than you think it ever could. I'm not exactly undertaking the Ironman Triathlon, where a group of ridiculously fit individuals having nothing better to do on a race day than undertake to swim 2.4 miles, then ride a bike for 112 miles and then run a full marathon, in that order and without a break. I am only playing the drums, after all, but at least the Ironman athletes have finished in 17 hours or so, and can all go to their beds. I have played 20 out of the last 21 days, on sometimes as little as four hours' sleep, and I still have another eight days left before I get a break.

After returning home from playing drums at the theatre, I climbed into the spare bed in an attempt to sleep through the rousing of the house at 6.00am when the children wake to go to school. As usual I was only partially successful in this endeavour, and I slumbered in and out of sleep with the sound of my children laughing, arguing, dropping things on the floor, picking them up, shouting from room to room, along with the accompanying audio of other early morning activities – mixed with my dream, which consisted of a Frenchman chasing me across flat rooftops. I really shouldn't eat cheese before I go to bed.

Tomorrow is a travel day: I am taking a flight to Amsterdam for the final two shows of The Moody Blues tour 2010.

**Postcard 56**

FOR CORRESPONDENCE     FOR ADDRESS ONLY

*Monday*
*September 27th*
*2010*

*London, UK*
*to*
*Amsterdam,*
*The Netherlands*

Serie 31  715.6.5

You will remember from yesterday's postcard that I was beginning to lament about being tired, and although I managed around seven hours' sleep last night, it certainly didn't feel like it at nine o'clock this morning. I know I'm not sick with a disease or some other infectious condition, but I certainly recognise that unless I get some serious rest, the symptoms suggesting that I am sick will continue.

My taxi arrived exactly on time, and after putting my case in the boot of the car and climbing into the back seat behind the driver, I fell fast asleep before we even reached the end of my road. I don't think the driver fully noticed my slumber, as he began recounting an anecdote about something, to this day I know not what. I emerged into consciousness as we approached the airport, with the driver still talking.

'And you will not believe what happened then.'

'What?' I replied, not knowing quite what was going on, or where I was.

He took my monosyllabic blurt as genuine interest, and continued: 'He gave me all the money back.'

I didn't have the heart to tell him I had not the faintest idea what he was talking about.

Being chauffeur-driven to an airport to catch a plane to fly to a city for an international concert is a bit different to catching the 163 from the end of the road. It must be something to do with the romantic notion of travelling to an exotic location – even if I'm not. Or it could be the intoxicating whiff of aviation fuel. Having said that, Amsterdam is one of my favourite cities in the world, and really is exotic.

The entrance to Terminal 5 normally puts a spring in my step similar to that of a triple espresso, but not on this occasion. I positively plodded along the newly tiled floor, pulling my suitcase, which was a hair's breadth beneath the maximum weight allowance for this short-haul flight and had only one working wheel. My computer rucksack was my carry-on bag, weighing slightly more than the suitcase, and it was pulling my shoulders down. I found I had to lean forward, stretching my forehead out in front of me as if attempting to head a ball into the back of a net, just to stay upright.

In a daze, I went through the process of checking in my heavy suitcase while trying to camouflage my oversized carry-on luggage from the lady issuing the ticket. As I was flying economy, I made a feeble attempt to be upgraded, asking in what I thought was a discreetly coded manner if there was 'any room at the front of the plane.' My scam was detected instantly, and in a very professional tone I was handed the economy boarding pass with the words, 'We already have a pilot, thank you.' Honestly, some people.

Continuing through the bothersome airport security, I went through the process of almost completely disrobing in order to pass through the metal detector without setting off the alarm. Personally I think they should devise some sort of bomb-proof room, which, when you enter, electronically detonates any hidden explosive device you may be concealing. If such a vestibule could be invented we would at least cut down on the number of semi-naked people at airport security.

My father, who lives in the US, visited me a few years ago in London. While he was over here I happened to put his coat on to go out to my car one day, and lost my keys down a small hole in his pocket. As I searched the lining of his coat I found a single round of ammunition from his Browning hunting rifle in the lining of his coat pocket – as you do. One day, when he was out in the woods, it had slid down there without him knowing. This was post-9/11, but it wasn't found until thousands of miles away from the Maine woods – after he had passed through three airport security systems. I don't want to imagine what would have happened if that had been discovered.

However, I digress. Once in the airport proper, I bought an expensive European plug adapter (it was one of the things I took out of my case in order to bring the weight below its allowance), and then medicated myself with caffeine in Pret a Manger. A very large frothy cappuccino was placed on the table in front of me, in a position where I could clearly see the departures screen, meaning I could comfortably sit in the same position until my gate was called. That was the plan, anyway.

After what seemed like a few seconds, I awakened from what felt like a deep sleep, my body slumped forward, with the froth from the now cold coffee against the tip of my nose ushering me back to consciousness, like one of those nodding dogs you see in the back of old cars on the motorway. I had slowly nose-dived the coffee cup during what turned out to be a full one-hour nap, and the final call for my gate was flashing in red neon on the departures screen.

Picking up my bag I began running in something more than slight panic, looking rather like a confused bull in a china shop – without checking which gate I was supposed to be running towards. After glancing at a passing screen without stopping, I managed to run to the opposite end of the terminal, and ended up having to ask for directions. Some ten minutes after the printed departure time, and mumbling things like, 'Oh, fuck it' under my breath, I arrived at the gate only to find my flight had been delayed, and I could actually board. I cannot tell you how happy this made me.

It's never nice being the last person to board a plane, especially those short haul ones where everyone can see you walk down the aisle. Of course they thought I was the reason for the delay, and if looks could kill I would have been at least severely wounded. I found my seat, which required two people – both firmly ensconced – to fold newspapers, move coats, lift up seat back tables and generally disrupt all within a three-row radius, in order for me to take my place. It didn't really matter, as I was once again fast asleep before take-off.

Amsterdam's Schiphol Airport is quite small considering it's an international airport, but this means I easily found my driver, who was nonchalantly waiting with a handwritten sign reading 'Marchal.' At least I think he was my driver; he was the only one with a sign phonetically resembling my name, so I just nodded at him – as you do – and we walked to his car. The 20-minute journey to the hotel was enormously entertaining, as I was fed continuously (and I mean continuously) quirky one-line jokes.

'What do they call a judge with no thumbs?'

'Er... I don't know.'

'Justice Fingers.'

After which the comedian-driver roared with laughter for a couple of minutes before apparently remembering another long-forgotten joke. I found myself shaking my head and chuckling away, despite the terrible delivery and rather incongruous venue.

'What did one snowman say to the other?'

'Er... again I don't know,' I offered.

'Do you smell carrots? Ha ha ha ha ha ha ha ha ha ha.'

'Ha, yes very funny... How much further?'

Before long we arrived at a rather nice hotel in the centre of Amsterdam. Entering my room, I discovered that the nice people in the hotel had installed UK-style wall plugs. So if anyone needs an expensive European adapter, please contact my publisher: I know of one going cheap. This is also the punch line to one of the jokes my driver told me about a budgie, but it's so bad I couldn't possible recount it here.

**Postcard 57**

FOR CORRESPONDENCE

FOR ADDRESS ONLY

Tuesday
September 28th and
Wednesday
September 29th
2010

Heineken Arena,
Amsterdam,
The Netherlands

Serie 97  H.4.5.8

Not far from the hotel is a rather lovely park called Vondelpark, and after breakfasting in the Café Max on Max Euweplein – my favourite café in all of Amsterdam – I took a leisurely stroll around the delightful 45 hectares that is Vondelpark. A statue of the eponymous Dutch poet Joost van den Vondel, dating back to 1867, is situated in the centre of the park. It (the park) was originally designed to be on the edge of the city, but as Amsterdam has sprawled outwards over the decades, it's now a central park; in fact it's Amsterdam's largest and most famous park, attracting about ten million visitors a year.

A stroll was all I could manage; I think a run or even a laggardly jog would have put me in hospital, the way I was feeling. This did not bode well for the final concerts of the tour. After my hearty and filling breakfast and a slow walk in the fresh air, I ambled back to the hotel and fell asleep... again. It didn't seem to matter how much sleep I was getting; I couldn't shake this feeling of fatigue, and I knew that come the evening I would once again be expecting my body to display energy and musical precision, regardless. So I stayed on my back for as long as possible, missing all the wonderful things the capital of the Netherlands has to offer – such as the Van Gogh Museum, the Rijksmuseum, the Rembrandt House Museum, and Anne Frank's House. Today, however, I felt about as useful as Anne Frank's drum kit, so I stayed in bed, horizontal until the lobby call.

The Heineken Arena in Amsterdam has always been a great gig for the Moodies. Sometimes a city just seems to click with a band, and this appears to be the case with Amsterdammers and The Moody Blues, so much so that we played there for two nights to a simply stunning reception. Unfortunately our wonderful Eat To The Beat travelling restaurant didn't make it to mainland Europe – they had another tour already booked, which meant we were left to the 'talents' of the local caterers. On this topic, I will skip a beat and move forward in order that I don't offend anyone.

For the longest time these final two concerts had been a distant point in the future, like the water beneath a ten metre diving board – it appears to be such a long way, yet within seconds you're crashing though it. Likewise these concerts had appeared on the horizon, and seemingly just as quickly, we were here and about to play them.

There is something truly amazing about performing. The old adage 'the show must go on' obviously derives from countless obstacles overcome, and I don't know any professional performer who doesn't live by this mantra. Noel Coward, however, famously queried the cliché in the early 1950s, by writing a song with the title *Why Must the Show Go On?* Nevertheless, it is tattooed much like graffiti across my consciousness, and as such I went through nothing short of a metamorphosis as I entered the building. My limbs instantly felt energetic, my mind became alert, and I was very quickly overtaken with the anticipation of performing, to what I knew would be a great crowd. Maybe it was my ego waking up? If it was, then I was grateful for it in this instance.

In high spirits, Justin, John, Graeme, Alan, Norda, Julie, Udo and I all squeezed and jostled into the small lift, which took us to the third floor dressing rooms. As I was standing against the wall of the lift, Julie gasped and blurted, 'Oh my God!' while looking at me.

For a split second it was a little disconcerting, as I had no idea what she was referring to. Had I got something hanging from my nose? Maybe my breakfast was still residing on my jacket? It turned out that there were pictures on the wall of all the artists that have performed here, and they were directly behind me. Apparently in one particular photograph, I was the spitting image of the lead singer from Big Country, as he screams into a microphone. It did actually look quite uncanny, so I mimicked his facial expression in front of the picture as Julie took a photo, to the delight of the occupants of the lift.

After some 'food' and one more short power nap, the final show was upon us. We all walked to the side of the stage, with the crowd buzzing. I walked up onto the platform and sat behind the drums with a feeling of electricity; could this really be the final venue of a year's touring with The Moody Blues? It had an 'end of school year' feel to it. All the pressure was off, and the body language of all on stage was relaxed and confident. The show began, and I sat back and viewed it almost from above. The crowd went wild as the introduction music faded, and the American-accented voice announced 'Ladieeees and

Gentlemen... The MOOOODY BLUUUUUES!'

I have to tell you (I may have said this before) that the novelty never, ever wears off. Any feelings of fatigue were totally gone, and I felt like an athlete completing a lap of honour. The sound in my ears was crystal clear, the drums popped and fizzed with energy, and I could see audience members who had travelled from all over the world just to catch the final two concerts. The mental roll call went on in my head as I clocked the eyes of one fan after another, all sitting or standing, bouncing along to the music. I didn't even have to think about what I was doing – it just happened before me. At one point John turned around and faced me as we both jammed together and beamed at each other as the groove played itself. This was musical heaven.

A physical tingling sensation accompanied me off the stage for the intermission, and I allowed myself an additional half-time Red Bull, as I didn't want to lose the buzz. This feeling is the reason I wanted to be a musician in the first place. I changed out of my already sweat-soaked clothes and donned a fresh outfit. As I walked back on for the second half, I began to wonder if the recently discarded wet stage clothes (which I will have to take home with me) would affect the weight of my case on the flight tomorrow, so I began the second half of the show with a mental inventory of my suitcase. Finding it difficult to shake this thought process, I momentarily became rather annoyed as it distracted me from enjoying the job at hand. My mind quickly changed to breakfast that morning...

'Oh come on, concentrate,' I said to myself.

My brain felt like a drunken monkey swinging from one branch of thought to another. The physicality of drumming very soon overcame any random thoughts and I was quickly back in the zone. The band moved up a gear to one I don't think we've engaged before, and I was having more fun now than during any activity I can remember ever taking part in.

This was becoming indubitably one of the most enjoyable playing experiences I could remember. The tour had been incontestably magnificent and we were finishing on a high. The end of the show came around too quickly for my liking, and I found myself walking to the front of the stage to take a bow. Alan grabbed my waist and pulled me in close to him, while John held my arm up from the wrist like the winner of a boxing match, and we all took a bow in this ad hoc embrace, to a standing ovation. This was a really potent experience.

And so with an exit-stage-left from the final concert, our travels for this year were over. Standing in the hot shower in the dressing room after the concert, knowing that the crew were breaking down the gear for the last time, and knowing that Julie and Alan would be flying to the US in a few hours, and everyone was moving on to the next thing in their lives, made for a momentary feeling of melancholy. We had been through so much together, and in the blink of an eye it was over.

After hurried goodbyes all round, we climbed in to some very plush vehicles taking us back to the hotel. I sat in the comfortable leather seat, looking through the rain-soaked window, watching the streets of Amsterdam speed by, with a feeling of exhaustion once more overcoming me. I was still oscillating between feeling match-fit and dreadful, and the end of the tour brought a sense of complete anticlimax.

On previous tours we have had all sorts of final-concert

gatherings, parties, and nights out. On some occasions they really have been 'rock 'n' roll' for all the right reasons. Tonight, however, I found myself completely exhausted and in my hotel room with no energy to even walk around the city to take in the wonderful night-time ambience. One thing that made me think I was not actually ill was that I couldn't stop eating. It didn't matter how much food I consumed; a few hours later I was ravenous, so I ordered eggs benedict with a glass of hot milk from room service. It was delicious.

**Postcard 58**

FOR CORRESPONDENCE     FOR ADDRESS ONLY

*Thursday*
*September 30th*
*2010*

*Amsterdam,*
*The Netherlands*
*to*
*London,*
*UK*

Waking up this morning after being on tour for what truly felt like an extended period of time, brought about an unusual, disjointed feeling. The everyday thoughts that had been pushed to the back of my brain over the previous weeks (money, commitments, family issues), suddenly advanced into the forefront of my mind like a tsunami, filling the void.

However, I was still officially on tour, because I had woken up in Amsterdam. Today the technical difficulties of packing my case with the items taken from the tour wardrobe, but keeping it under the weight limit of 28 kilos, were foremost in my mind.

Alan and Julie were already on their way home, as they left the hotel at 5.00am to get to the airport. That had to hurt. John, Justin and Graeme were flying to various parts of the globe, and Norda and I were flying back to London on the same flight later in the day. This meant I was able to ease myself into the day in a relatively civilized manner. Gripping the final opportunity to wake up without an alarm or wake-up call from the front desk was a treat this morning, because when I am home and 'real life' kicks in, the alarm will be going off every morning, and I will be getting up like a regular person. I am about to experience re-entry. On this occasion, returning home having been at home already during the UK tour will just add to the discombobulation.

It was raining heavily across most of Europe, and Amsterdam was clearly getting its share, so I borrowed a huge and lovely red umbrella from the front desk – the sort that makes you feel rather affluent when you walk around with it open. I walked over the bridge towards my favourite café, looking in all directions in order not to become intertwined with any advancing bicycles. Amsterdam has countless thousands of them, and if you are not completely on your guard, at some point you will be hit.

On the previous Moody Blues visit to this city, I was walking around with the then Moodies keyboard player and my very good friend, Paul Bliss. Paul is capable of the fastest witty retorts, known as 'Blissiles' to his friends. On that tour I was twice hit head-on by good-looking girls on bikes; the first time I was completely knocked over. The second time, I was impaled on the bike as the rider also fell off. As we disentwined ourselves from each other, I couldn't help but notice that she was particularly attractive. Without either of us saying a word and while Paul stood there observing, she got back on the bike and carried on as if nothing had happened. As she rode off Paul and I stood next to each other, shoulder-to-shoulder, like statues, motionless, watching this vision of loveliness pedal off into the distance.

'Why is it that only beautiful women crash into me?' I said hoping for some ego-feeding cryptic response.

While still looking in the direction of the now long-gone cyclist, Paul said, 'Because you're invisible to them, Gordon.'

I enjoyed meandering through an adagio morning, and managed to negotiate the short distance from hotel to Café Max and back again, on this occasion without any major incidents. A big breakfast of smoked salmon and scrambled eggs, on thick homemade toasted bread with a large steaming cappuccino, was the perfect final breakfast of the tour.

My suitcase, which now had a flute, a practice pad and some two sets of wet stage clothes in it, was proving a problem weight-wise. Now decidedly over the limit, I stood in my hotel room contemplating the luggage as if the simple act of staring at it would somehow make it weigh less. Incredibly I managed to fit even more items into my computer rucksack, and when I put it on in the hotel room, to take a look at myself in the mirror to see what I looked like (you know, like you do), I decided I would not look out of place walking along the northeast ridge of Everest.

Admittedly, in an attempt to transfer as much as possible from my luggage to my person, I had on a lot of clothes. I was wearing my North Face padded coat, under which I had, in order: a thick hoodie, a jumper, a checked lumberjack shirt, and two T-shirts; also a pair of combat jeans, and Timberland boots. I looked ridiculous, but I managed to get my luggage to the exact weight. When I met Norda in the lobby, she looked at me curiously as I waddled through reception like the Michelin man dressed for a very cold day.

I arrived home in the early evening just as it was getting dark. My taxi dropped me off outside the house, and I could see the lights inside. As I walked to the front door I spotted the Disney Channel on the television through the lounge window, and I knew my youngest daughter (out of sight) would be reclining on the couch, and Harley, our dog, would be on her lap, even though she's officially not allowed on the furniture (Harley, that is). I paused for a moment before turning the key, and looked through the frosted glass of the front door, to see my eldest daughter run down the stairs in her gymnastics leotard. I felt a glow inside as I soaked in the familial warmth of the house. I turned the key and opened the door; the smell of my wife's home cooking and fresh-baked bread instantly entered my nostrils. I heard the dog bark and my daughters shout the words 'Daddy's home!' Rock 'n' roll.

# Thank you

It wasn't until I sat down to write a thank you to all the people that have contributed and helped me with this book, that I realised what a huge backup system I am lucky enough to have. Some of the people below are so important that the book could not have been written without them; others are part of a support structure that make the writing of a book like this possible. Everyone mentioned - in some way, shape or form - has played a part and it is with the deepest gratitude that I offer my sincerest appreciation to:

The Moody Blues: Justin Hayward, John Lodge, Ray Thomas and my compatriot on drums and author of the foreword to this book, Graeme Edge. I have been lucky enough to work alongside these legendary musicians for the past 23 years and they gave their blessing for me to write about being on tour with them. Without them these words simply would not be written.

Alan Hewitt, Julie Ragins and Norda Mullen, my fellow backing musicians and Udo Wolf, our Glorious Leader, sometimes referred to as our tour manager, all of whom make the whole process of touring enjoyable beyond belief. Mark Hogue, Allan Terry, Russell Achzet, Mick Thornton, Karen Colvin and all of the crew.

Jamie Franklin and Jules Tabberer-Stewart at Roland UK (for the amazing TD30). Garrison at DW drums (for my beautiful handmade drum kit). Jay Medynski at Regal Tip (for all my drum sticks). Bob Boos at Sabian (for the best sounding cymbals). Also thank you to Andy Stinson for your insightful and priceless advice at the very beginning of this project.

Steve Clark, Shoba Vazirani and Annabel Silk at Splendid Books for having faith in me as a writer and then backing it up with a passion that took me quite by surprise. Also Marcos D'Cruze who saw this coming before anyone... he always does.

My brother Robert, who is a constant and never ending feed of enthusiasm and clarity - I don't know what I would do without him.

My dear friend Paul Bliss (who toured with me for 20 years with The Moody Blues, and is like a brother to me) and my best mate Andy Holdsworth, the most talented photographer I know, who is responsible for most of the photographs in this book.

My other family, Alan and Audrey, and Howard Wilson, who have supported me through decades of turmoil and created a level emotional playing field for me to bounce around on while trying to be a 'creative.'

Finally, and most importantly, to my wife Susan, who knows exactly what I'm like and remarkably still loves me and my two daughters Phoebe and Frankie, who are quite simply the meaning of life itself.

# More from
## Splendid Books

### A Greater Love
*By Olga Watkins with James Gillespie*

When the Gestapo seize 20-year-old Olga Czepf's fiancé she is determined to find him and sets off on an extraordinary 2,000-mile search across Nazi-occupied Europe risking betrayal, arrest and death.

As the Second World War heads towards its bloody climax, she refuses to give up – even when her mission leads her to the gates of Dachau and Buchenwald concentration camps...

*'A book that deserves to be read'* **Daily Mail**

*'An incredible story of love against the odds'* **Daily Express**
**£7.99 (paperback)**

### Catching Bullets : Memoirs of a Bond Fan
*By Mark O'Connell*

From the offbeat vantage point of a gay teenager whose grandfather was chauffeur to legendary 007 producer Cubby Broccoli, Catching Bullets : Memoirs of a Bond Fan is a love-letter to James Bond, Duran Duran title songs and bolting down your tea quick enough to watch Roger Moore falling out of a plane without a parachute.

When Jimmy O'Connell took a job as chauffeur for 007 producers Eon Productions, it would not just be Cubby Broccoli, Roger Moore and Sean Connery he would drive to James Bond. His grandson Mark swiftly hitches a metaphorical ride on a humorous journey of filmic discovery where Bond movies fire like bespoke bullets at a Reagan-era Catholic childhood marked with divorce, a closet-gay adolescence sound-tracked by John Barry and an adult life as a comedy writer still inspired by that Broccoli movie magic.
**£7.99 (paperback)**

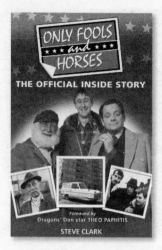

## Only Fools and Horses - The Official Inside Story
*By Steve Clark, Foreword by Theo Paphitis*

This book takes us behind the scenes to reveal the secrets of the hit show and is fully authorised by the family of its writer John Sullivan.

This engaging tribute contains interviews with the show's stars and members of the production team, together with rarely seen pictures.

Written by bestselling author Steve Clark, the only writer on set for the filming of *Only Fools and Horses*, *The Green Green Grass* and *Rock & Chips*, this book gives a fascinating and unique insight into this legendary series.
**£9.99 (paperback)**

## The Official Only Fools and Horses Quiz Book
*Compiled by Dan Sullivan and Jim Sullivan, Foreword by John Sullivan*

Now you can test your knowledge of the legendary sitcom in *The Official Only Fools and Horses Quiz Book*, which is packed with more than 1,000 brain-teasers about the show.

Plus there's an episode guide and an exclusive foreword by the show's creator and writer John Sullivan, who reveals some of the mystery behind the much-loved series and just how he came up with some of television's most memorable moments.
**£7.99 (paperback)**

## The Wit and Wisdom of Only Fools and Horses
*Compiled by Dan Sullivan, Foreword by Sir David Jason OBE*

The crème de menthe of the hilarious one-liners from *Only Fools and Horses* have been brought together for the first time in *The Wit and Wisdom of Only Fools and Horses*. Re-live all Del, Rodney, Grandad, Uncle Albert, Boycie, Trigger and the rest of the gang's funniest and most memorable lines.

Compiled by Dan Sullivan, son of *Only Fools and Horses* creator John Sullivan, and with a Foreword by Sir David Jason OBE, this triffic book is a lovely jubbly, pukka, 42-carat gold-plated bargain.
**£4.99 (paperback)**

### The British Television Location Guide
*By Steve Clark and Shoba Vazirani*

This beautifully illustrated book reveals the settings for dozens of top television shows. From *Downton Abbey* to *Doc Martin* and from *Midsomer Murders* to *Doctor Who*, the book gives details of how you can visit the places you have seen so many times on television. It includes details of the locations for more than 100 television series.
**Just £9.99 (full colour paperback)**

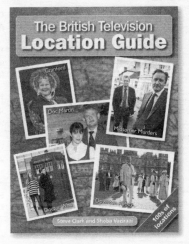

### On The Beat
*By Graham Cole*

This is the warm, witty and frank autobiography of Graham Cole, who played PC Tony Stamp in the long-running police drama series *The Bill*. It's a great read – and reveals the real story of life behind the scenes at *The Bill*.
**£9.99 (hardback) or £7.99 (paperback)**

### An East End Life
*By Derek Martin*

This is the fascinating real East End life story of actor Derek Martin who starred as Charlie Slater in *EastEnders*. From growing up during the Blitz to starring in the hit soap, it's a frank and fearless autobiography.
**£9.99 (hardback)**

**Splendid**
BOOKS

**www.splendidbooks.co.uk**
**www.facebook.com/splendidbooks**

If you enjoyed this book please "Like" it on
Facebook
**www.facebook.com/postcardsfrom**

**Follow us on Twitter @splendidbooks**